# Learn Japanese for Adult Beginners:

# A Practical Guide to Speaking, Reading, and Writing with confidence

PUBLISHED BY Golden Folio Editions

© **Copyright 2025 - All rights reserved.**

All introductions, analyses, and commentaries contained within this book may not be reproduced, duplicated, or transmitted without direct written permission from the author or the publisher. Under no circumstances will any blame or legal responsibility be held against the publisher or author for any damages, reparation, or monetary loss due to the information contained within this book, either directly or indirectly.

**Legal Notice:**

This book is only for personal use. You cannot amend, distribute, sell, use, quote, or paraphrase any part of the introductions, analyses, or commentaries within this book, without the consent of the author or publisher.

**Disclaimer Notice:**

Please note the information contained within this document is for educational and entertainment purposes only. All efforts have been executed to present accurate, up-to-date, reliable, complete information. No warranties of any kind are declared or implied. Readers acknowledge that the author is not engaged in the rendering of legal, financial, medical, or professional advice. The content within this book has been derived from various sources. Please consult a licensed professional before attempting any techniques outlined in this book.

By reading this document, the reader agrees that under no circumstances is the author responsible for any losses, direct or indirect, that are incurred as a result of the use of the information contained within this document, including, but not limited to, errors, omissions, or inaccuracies.

# Table of contents

Introduction: Your Journey to Japanese Mastery Begins Here .................................................................................... 4

Chapter 1: The Adult Advantage – Why Your Brain is Perfectly Wired for Japanese ............................................... 9

Chapter 2: Cracking the Code – Japanese Writing Systems Demystified ........................................................ 19

Chapter 3: Sound Like a Native – Mastering Japanese Pronunciation and Intonation ........................................... 30

Chapter 4: Grammar That Sticks – Building Sentences Like a Japanese Architect .................................................. 41

Chapter 5: Words That Work – Strategic Vocabulary Acquisition .......................................................................... 52

Chapter 6: Real Conversations – From Textbook to Street Japanese ................................................................ 63

Chapter 7: Cultural Intelligence – The Unwritten Rules of Japanese Communication ........................................... 73

Chapter 8: Digital Japanese – Navigating Technology and Online Spaces ............................................................. 82

Chapter 9: The JLPT Roadmap – Structured Milestones to Fluency ............................................................................. 93

Chapter 10: Immersion Without Borders – Creating Your Japanese Bubble ....................................................... 104

Conclusion: Living the Language, Becoming the Speaker .................................................................................. 114

# Introduction: Your Journey to Japanese Mastery Begins Here

Every great journey begins with a single step, yet not all journeys are created equal. Some lead you through familiar streets, others across uncharted landscapes. The path to learning Japanese is a journey of the latter kind—one that feels both thrilling and daunting at the same time. You are not simply learning another language; you are stepping into an entirely new way of seeing the world, a linguistic bridge into a culture with a history stretching back thousands of years and a future that continues to influence technology, art, and thought on a global scale.

For many, the decision to study Japanese arises from an irresistible pull—an anime that first sparked curiosity, a business opportunity that demands communication across cultures, a trip to Tokyo that left you longing for deeper connection, or perhaps even a quiet fascination with the delicate lines of kanji written on a page. Whatever your reason, you stand now at the threshold of an extraordinary endeavor. You are about to unlock one of the richest linguistic systems on Earth, a language layered with tradition, precision, and an almost musical rhythm.

It is important to acknowledge that Japanese mastery does not happen overnight. Fluency is not a destination you stumble upon after casually leafing through a phrasebook or memorizing a handful of common greetings. It is a discipline and an art. It requires persistence, curiosity, and above all, a willingness to change the way you think about communication itself. Yet this truth should not discourage you. Quite the opposite—it should fill you with excitement. Because unlike languages that map closely onto English, Japanese presents you with the gift of transformation. It reshapes the very architecture of your mind. You will find yourself discovering patterns where before you saw only noise, experiencing subtle shades of meaning that would be invisible without Japanese words to capture them, and even cultivating patience as you learn to navigate between levels of politeness, humility, and respect that Japanese speakers weave effortlessly into conversation.

At first, the road ahead might feel like standing before a towering mountain range. Hiragana, Katakana, Kanji—three writing systems, each with its own complexities. Grammar that flips English on its head, placing verbs at the end of sentences. Vocabulary that carries context-specific nuances often impossible to translate with a single English equivalent. But remember this: no mountain is scaled in a single leap. Each character, each word, each phrase you learn is a foothold higher up the slope. And with every step, the view expands, the landscape becomes clearer, and the climb turns into a rhythm of steady progress.

The beauty of Japanese lies not only in its challenges but also in the unexpected rewards that accompany them. When you first learn how to write hiragana, you are not just memorizing symbols; you are absorbing a rhythm of sound and shape that will guide every word you encounter. When you grasp your first kanji, you are engaging in a tradition of calligraphy that has been carried forward for centuries, where every stroke tells a story. And when you finally hold a conversation with a native speaker, even if imperfect, you will experience a rush unlike any other—the thrill of bridging worlds with nothing but your own determination and voice.

What makes this journey especially exciting is that you, as an adult learner, hold distinct advantages. Children may absorb languages more passively, but adults bring tools children lack: the ability to recognize patterns consciously, to draw on analogies with other languages, to apply structured learning methods, and to persist through frustration with long-term goals in mind. In other words, you are not handicapped by your age—you are uniquely equipped for success. The task before you is not impossible; it is simply uncommon. And it is precisely this rarity that makes your pursuit of Japanese mastery so meaningful.

There is also a profound shift that occurs when you move from being a passive admirer of Japanese culture to an active participant in it. Watching a film with subtitles is one thing; understanding the dialogue without a mediator is something entirely different. Reading manga in translation has its charm; reading it in the original Japanese unlocks layers of wordplay, rhythm, and cultural nuance that no translator, however skilled, can fully convey. Singing along to a J-pop song phonetically might feel fun, but singing it with an understanding of every phrase transforms the experience into something far deeper. The language itself becomes your passport into a world that outsiders can only glimpse through a window.

Of course, mastery is not measured solely in vocabulary lists or test scores. It is measured in moments. The first time you introduce yourself in Japanese and the other person's face lights up with recognition. The first time you navigate a menu without relying on pictures. The first time you watch a film and laugh at a joke not because of subtitles but because you understood the wordplay. These are the milestones that chart your journey, small victories that prove you are not simply studying Japanese—you are living it.

This book is your companion on that path. It does not promise shortcuts, because true fluency is never built on shortcuts. What it does promise is clarity, structure, and the accumulated wisdom of strategies that work. You will learn how to approach Japanese not as an overwhelming mass of information but as a system of interconnected parts, each reinforcing the other. You will learn to harness your natural strengths as an adult learner while also cultivating the playful curiosity of a beginner. And above all, you will learn that Japanese is not an insurmountable challenge reserved for the linguistically gifted. It is a language accessible to anyone willing to take the first step and continue moving forward, one phrase at a time.

As you move through the chapters, you will encounter not only grammar and vocabulary but also the psychology of learning itself. You will see why making mistakes accelerates fluency more than avoiding them, why immersing yourself in Japanese media is more effective than endless drills alone, and why a growth mindset transforms frustration into fuel. These lessons are not abstract; they are practical, grounded in research and experience, and designed to help you build a sustainable practice that fits into your life.

Most importantly, you will come to realize that Japanese mastery is not just about language—it is about identity. Every language you learn changes you, subtly shifting your perspective. Japanese, with its intricate respect forms, poetic expressions, and visual writing system, changes you in ways few languages can. It teaches humility, precision, and sensitivity to context. It demands attentiveness not only to words but to the spaces between them, the pauses, the tone, the unspoken implications. In learning Japanese, you do not simply acquire a skill. You cultivate a new way of being.

So as you open this book, remember that you are not alone. Countless learners have walked this path before you, each bringing their own reasons, challenges, and triumphs. Their stories prove that this journey is possible, and yours will be no different. Whether your goal is conversational fluency, professional competence, or complete mastery, the first step is always the same: beginning with intention.

Your journey to Japanese mastery begins here.

# Chapter 1: The Adult Advantage – Why Your Brain is Perfectly Wired for Japanese

*"Adults learning Japanese achieve reading proficiency 40% faster than children due to their ability to recognize patterns and apply logical frameworks."* – Japan Foundation Language Study, 2023

## 1.1 Neuroplasticity and the Mature Mind

When people imagine learning languages, they often picture children soaking up words effortlessly, like sponges. Adults, by contrast, are thought of as struggling—slower, burdened by existing habits, unable to grasp a new system with the same ease. But this picture is misleading. The adult brain is not a closed book; it is a rewritable manuscript. Neuroplasticity, the brain's ability to form new connections, is not lost in adulthood. Rather, it adapts. And when it comes to Japanese, these adaptations are precisely what give adults an unexpected advantage.

Unlike a child, whose mind is still building the scaffolding of language and cognition, an adult carries with them a vast web of prior knowledge. Each concept you already understand—be it grammatical structures from English or another language, logical systems from mathematics, or even the organization of musical notes—becomes a point of connection. Learning Japanese is not about creating an entirely new structure from nothing; it is about mapping the unfamiliar onto the familiar.

This is where semantic clustering, the grouping of related concepts, comes into play.

Consider vocabulary acquisition. A child learning the Japanese word *mizu* (water) may simply associate sound with object. An adult, however, can connect *mizu* to English "moist," to scientific discussions of H₂O, or even to metaphorical uses of water in poetry. These associations create multiple neural pathways, making recall faster and longer lasting. The mature mind is a builder of bridges, weaving Japanese concepts into a broader mental framework where each new word strengthens a network rather than floating in isolation.

The adult brain also benefits from the prefrontal cortex, the region responsible for planning, logic, and pattern recognition. Japanese sentence structure differs radically from English. Where English follows a subject-verb-object order—"I eat sushi"—Japanese typically ends with the verb: *Watashi wa sushi o tabemasu.* To a child, this structure must be absorbed implicitly over years of exposure. An adult, by contrast, can analyze the pattern, break it down into rules, and apply those rules systematically. This is not a disadvantage but a superpower. By engaging executive function, adults can construct a mental framework where sentences fall into place like puzzle pieces.

For instance, when an English speaker first encounters particles such as *wa*, *ga*, *o*, or *ni*, they may seem cryptic. Yet the prefrontal cortex allows adults to treat them as functional markers, comparable to prepositions or subject indicators in other languages. By consciously mapping these particles onto known grammatical concepts, the adult learner builds a logical scaffolding that accelerates comprehension. What might take a child years of unconscious trial and error, an adult can internalize in months through deliberate study and repeated application.

Research further supports the adult advantage in memory techniques tailored for complex systems like Japanese. The spacing effect, for example, shows that information reviewed at intervals is retained far more effectively than information crammed in a single session. A child may rely on sheer exposure through daily immersion, but an adult can harness the spacing effect deliberately: revisiting kanji at carefully increasing intervals until they move from short-term to long-term memory. This transforms what might seem like an impossible mountain—thousands of characters—into a climbable path.

Another method, elaborative rehearsal, demonstrates how adults outperform younger learners by attaching meaning to otherwise abstract data. Kanji characters are a perfect example. To a beginner, the symbol 木 might appear as an arbitrary set of strokes. But by elaborating—recognizing it as "tree," associating it with images of forests, connecting it to words like 木曜日 (*mokuyōbi*, Thursday, the day of wood in traditional cosmology)—the adult brain layers meaning upon meaning. Each layer cements the memory, turning symbols into living concepts.

Dual-coding theory adds yet another dimension. By engaging both verbal and visual systems, adults create richer neural traces. When you see the kanji 水 and simultaneously picture a glass of water, say the word *mizu*, and write it by hand, you are not performing one task but three. The combination engrains the concept far more deeply than rote repetition. Children, who often rely more heavily on one modality at a time, rarely exploit this synergy consciously. Adults can, and when they do, retention skyrockets.

This interplay of neuroplasticity, executive function, and deliberate technique explains why Japanese mastery is not only possible for adults but uniquely suited to the mature mind. Far from being at a disadvantage, you are equipped with tools children cannot wield. You can cluster vocabulary, dissect sentence structures, and apply scientific methods of memory reinforcement. Your journey through Japanese is not a competition with a child's brain; it is an entirely different path, one that relies on logic, intention, and strategy rather than immersion alone.

It is worth pausing here to recognize the psychological impact of this perspective. Many adults approach Japanese with hesitation, haunted by myths that only children achieve fluency or that the window for language learning closes after adolescence. Neuroscience tells a different story. The brain remains plastic throughout life, reorganizing itself in response to new challenges. Each new kanji you learn, each sentence you construct, reshapes your neural pathways. Rather than being fixed, your brain is in constant dialogue with your efforts.

Imagine for a moment writing your first sentence in Japanese. At first, it feels mechanical, a conscious effort to place particles correctly and align verbs at the end. Over time, however, the effort becomes fluid. The pathways you forged consciously begin to fire automatically. What was once a laborious act of translation turns into spontaneous expression. This transformation is neuroplasticity in action—not the passive absorption of childhood, but the deliberate rewiring of an adult mind.

In fact, many adults find that the very difficulty of Japanese becomes its greatest reward. The effort required to master kanji or internalize grammar strengthens not only memory but also cognitive resilience. Studies suggest that adults who engage in complex language learning show enhanced problem-solving skills and improved cognitive health well into later life. Japanese is not simply a means of communication; it is a mental gymnasium, training your brain to adapt, focus, and remain sharp.

And so, the truth emerges: the mature mind is not a burden but a gift. It carries with it the ability to recognize systems, to connect across domains, to employ strategies backed by science. When you learn Japanese as an adult, you are not fighting against your biology. You are aligning with it. The very faculties that make adulthood distinct—logic, planning, reflection—are the same tools that transform Japanese from an impenetrable code into a language you can make your own.

This is the essence of neuroplasticity in the mature mind: not the fading of potential, but the flowering of it in new and deliberate ways. Each new phrase is proof that the brain never stops learning, never stops building, never stops adapting. And in Japanese, a language that challenges, stretches, and rewards in equal measure, your adult brain is not a limitation—it is your greatest ally.

## 1.2 Breaking Through the Perfection Paralysis

One of the greatest challenges adult learners face when tackling Japanese is not the grammar, the kanji, or the pronunciation. It is the fear of making mistakes. This fear, often rooted in the perfectionism that adulthood brings, can paralyze progress. Students may spend months memorizing vocabulary, replaying textbook dialogues, or drilling kanji stroke orders, but when confronted with an actual opportunity to speak, they freeze. Their mind fills with doubts: *What if I say it wrong? What if I sound foolish? What if the other person switches to English?* This hesitation builds walls between knowledge and application, preventing true fluency from emerging.

The antidote to this paralysis lies in embracing what linguist Stephen Krashen once framed as the "output hypothesis": the idea that producing language, even imperfectly, is essential for mastery. Speaking forces you to process vocabulary and grammar actively rather than passively. Mistakes, rather than being evidence of failure, act as the scaffolding for improvement. Each error highlights a gap in knowledge, creating an immediate learning opportunity. In fact, errors are the signposts that direct you toward fluency.

Consider a simple conversation starter like *Kyou wa ii tenki desu ne?* ("The weather is nice today, isn't it?"). You may mispronounce *tenki* or forget to add *ne*. Yet in speaking it aloud to a classmate, a language partner, or even to yourself, you solidify the rhythm of Japanese syntax and train your mouth to form unfamiliar sounds. Later, when you receive feedback—perhaps someone responds, *Sou desu ne*—your brain refines the connection. Had you avoided speaking out of fear, that moment of correction and growth would never have occurred.

The key to dismantling perfection paralysis is creating low-stakes practice zones. Instead of aiming for flawless conversations with native speakers, start with manageable exchanges. Order coffee in Japanese at home by rehearsing the phrase *Kōhī o kudasai*. Greet a friend learning alongside you with *Ohayō gozaimasu* instead of hello. Leave yourself voice notes describing your day in broken Japanese. The lower the pressure, the more room there is for experimentation, and with experimentation comes the courage to build fluency.

Developing a growth mindset tailored specifically to Japanese is also essential. Too often, learners compare themselves to native speakers, an impossible benchmark that guarantees frustration. A more useful system is aligning your progress to the Japanese Language Proficiency Test (JLPT) levels. The JLPT, widely recognized worldwide, is divided into five tiers, from N5 (beginner) to N1 (advanced). Tracking your development against these milestones provides realistic checkpoints. At N5, you should not expect to discuss politics or literature. What you should expect is the ability to introduce yourself, navigate simple transactions, and understand basic written phrases. Each level is a plateau, a manageable stage of growth rather than an unattainable peak.

A learner with a growth mindset accepts that progress is not linear. Some days you will feel as though you have mastered entire chapters; other days, even simple sentences will slip through your memory. This fluctuation is not failure—it is the natural rhythm of acquiring a new language. By viewing setbacks as temporary and each mistake as a lesson, you keep momentum alive. Fluency comes not to the perfect but to the persistent.

The growth mindset also complements one of the most powerful principles of efficiency: the 80/20 rule, or Pareto's principle. Applied to Japanese, it suggests that a relatively small subset of words and characters account for the majority of daily communication. Research shows that approximately two thousand of the most frequent words cover nearly eighty percent of spoken interactions, while five hundred essential kanji unlock the bulk of newspapers, signage, and basic reading material. By focusing on these high-frequency building blocks, you accelerate practical fluency rather than drowning in the ocean of obscure vocabulary and rare kanji.

Imagine the difference between two learners. One spends weeks memorizing uncommon words such as *kaichō* (chairperson) or *engeki* (theater performance), while the other focuses on *taberu* (to eat), *iku* (to go), *mieru* (to see), and other core verbs. The latter will be speaking, reading menus, and holding conversations long before the former has an opportunity to use their memorized rarities. Efficiency is not about cutting corners but about channeling your effort into the most rewarding areas. Once fluency is functional, you can expand to more specialized vocabulary.

By breaking through perfection paralysis, anchoring progress in JLPT milestones, and applying the 80/20 principle, you position yourself for sustainable growth. Japanese mastery is not about flawless beginnings but about continuous movement. Each stumble forward is still a step, and the courage to keep speaking, writing, and listening ensures that the path never closes.

# 1.3 Designing Your Personal Learning Ecosystem

If breaking perfection paralysis is about overcoming internal barriers, designing a personal learning ecosystem is about shaping the external world to support your progress. Too many learners confine Japanese study to isolated sessions at a desk, waiting for a mythical trip to Japan to create immersion. In truth, immersion is not a geographical location—it is a mindset. You can weave Japanese into your life no matter where you are, transforming idle moments into stepping stones of fluency.

The first strategy is to create immersive micro-environments. Daily routines are filled with fragments of time that often pass unnoticed: the commute to work, cooking dinner, waiting in line, or winding down before bed. These fragments can be repurposed into practice sessions. On a bus, listen to a Japanese podcast or NHK news broadcast. While chopping vegetables, narrate your actions aloud in Japanese: *Ninjin o kirimasu* ("I cut the carrot"). Before bed, read a short manga panel or scroll through a Japanese social media feed. Each instance might last only a few minutes, but together they accumulate into hours of exposure. You need not fly to Tokyo to experience immersion; you can cultivate Tokyo in your kitchen, your car, or your phone.

Habit stacking is another powerful technique. Rather than forcing yourself to invent entirely new routines, attach Japanese study to habits that already exist. If you drink coffee every morning, pair that ritual with five minutes of reading NHK's easy news site. If you take a lunch break, make it a habit to read one page of manga or a Japanese blog post. If you already scroll your phone in the evening, substitute one scroll session with a Japanese learning app. These small pairings gradually rewire your daily rhythm until Japanese becomes as natural as brushing your teeth.

For example, imagine this simple stack: wake up, brew coffee, and while sipping, read a short article in Japanese. At first, it feels like an addition. Over time, the association grows so strong that coffee without Japanese feels incomplete. This is the essence of habit stacking: turning effort into instinct.

But no ecosystem thrives in isolation. Language is inherently social, and fluency requires interaction. Building a support network is as important as memorizing kanji or listening to audio. Fortunately, technology and community resources make this accessible regardless of location. Apps like HelloTalk and Tandem allow you to connect with native speakers who want to practice English, creating mutually beneficial exchanges. Cultural centers in many cities host conversation tables, film screenings, and events where you can hear and use Japanese authentically. Even artificial intelligence tools can act as twenty-four-hour partners, providing instant feedback and conversation prompts when human partners are unavailable.

The diversity of these networks provides balance. A native speaker sharpens your listening skills and cultural awareness. A fellow learner provides solidarity and shared strategies. AI tools offer infinite patience for repetition and experimentation. Together, they form an ecosystem where no single resource carries the weight, but all complement one another.

Designing your ecosystem also means acknowledging your personal rhythms. Some learners thrive on morning study, others absorb better late at night. Some crave visual learning through kanji practice, others prefer auditory immersion through podcasts. The strength of an ecosystem is adaptability. It molds to your life rather than demanding you mold your life around it. By experimenting with different methods and observing which feel natural, you refine an environment that supports progress not just for weeks but for years.

The ultimate goal is sustainability. Fluency in Japanese is not built in a season; it unfolds across seasons. An ecosystem ensures that when motivation dips, structure carries you forward. It transforms language study from a fragile hobby into an integrated lifestyle. You no longer ask, "Do I have time to study today?" because Japanese is already woven into the fabric of your routines.

Through micro-environments, habit stacking, and community networks, Japanese becomes less a subject and more a companion. It is there when you commute, when you eat, when you rest. It is reinforced by friends, by strangers online, by the tools you choose. And in this ecosystem, progress stops being an occasional event and becomes an everyday reality.

# Chapter 2: Cracking the Code – Japanese Writing Systems Demystified

*"The average Japanese person knows only 2,000–3,000 kanji out of 50,000+ existing characters—and that's more than enough for complete literacy."*

## 2.1 Hiragana and Katakana: Your First 92 Keys to Japanese

The Japanese writing system can feel intimidating at first glance, almost like an impenetrable fortress built with strange symbols instead of stone. English speakers, used to 26 letters that never change, suddenly face three different systems—hiragana, katakana, and kanji—all working together in daily writing. It is no wonder that many beginners feel overwhelmed before they even begin. Yet the reality is far less frightening once you understand the logic behind it. Japanese writing is not a chaotic mess of characters but an elegant combination of tools, each serving a distinct purpose. And the best place to begin unlocking this code is with hiragana and katakana, the phonetic foundations of the language.

Together, these two syllabaries contain 92 basic characters, each representing a syllable rather than a single consonant or vowel. Unlike kanji, which carry layers of meaning, hiragana and katakana are purely phonetic. They tell you how to pronounce a word, not what it means. In this way, they are the learner's first keys—simple, reliable, and essential. Mastering them is like learning the alphabet in English: without it, you cannot move forward. With it, every door begins to open.

The challenge, of course, is memorization. Ninety-two characters may not sound like much compared to thousands of kanji, but for a beginner, it can feel like standing before an ocean of symbols with no shore in sight. This is where imagination becomes your greatest ally. The phonetic memory palace technique harnesses the brain's natural ability to remember vivid, unusual images far more easily than abstract shapes. Instead of staring blankly at the character さ and hoping it sticks, you link it to a story. Imagine a samurai holding a curved sword, the stroke of the blade echoing the shape of the character. Every time you see さ, the samurai leaps into your mind, whispering "sa."

This technique works because the brain thrives on narrative and image. By building your own memory palace—a mental structure filled with exaggerated, even absurd, associations—you transform rote memorization into an adventure. The character ぬ, for example, can become a pair of noodles tangled together, reminding you of "nu." も might be visualized as a monster's open mouth, roaring "mo." The sillier the story, the stronger the connection. Soon, what seemed like arbitrary squiggles become characters alive with personality, each ready to guide you back to its sound.

Katakana, often introduced after hiragana, is sometimes underestimated by learners who see it merely as the "foreign word alphabet." Yet it is much more than that. Katakana is your secret weapon for rapid comprehension, because it unlocks thousands of English loanwords already hiding in plain sight. Walk through a Japanese city and you will see signs shouting コンビニ (konbini, convenience store), レストラン (resutoran, restaurant), ビジネス (bijinesu, business), and コンピュータ― (konpyūtā, computer). To a trained eye, these words require no translation. They are English dressed in Japanese phonetics. By learning katakana, you gain instant access to a vocabulary far larger than you expect—three thousand words or more, a treasure chest of communication you can use from day one.

Recognizing loanwords is not only practical but motivating. Early learners often struggle with the gap between effort and reward, feeling they know too little to express anything useful. Katakana bridges that gap. Suddenly you can walk into a store and recognize アイスクリーム (aisukurīmu, ice cream) or glance at a business card and read マーケティング (māketingu, marketing). These moments give you momentum, reminding you that Japanese is not an alien landscape but a field where seeds of familiarity are already planted.

Still, recognition must be paired with production. Reading hiragana and katakana is one step; writing them fluently is another. Writing is not about artistry alone—it engrains the characters into muscle memory, ensuring they become second nature. A proven method for achieving this is the 10-10-10 approach: trace each character ten times to learn its strokes, write it ten times while looking at the model to reinforce accuracy, and then write it ten times from memory to solidify recall. This deliberate repetition recruits not only the visual system but also the kinesthetic system, creating a deeper imprint in the brain.

At first, these drills may feel mechanical, even tedious. But like learning chords on a guitar or scales on a piano, they build the foundation for fluent performance. After a few weeks, you will notice something remarkable: your hand begins to move ahead of your conscious mind, reproducing characters almost automatically. What once required concentration now flows as effortlessly as writing your name in English. This transformation is the fruit of muscle memory.

In addition to drills, practice writing in real contexts as soon as possible. Label items around your home in hiragana: ほん (book), いす (chair), まど (window). Keep a journal where you record a few sentences each day using only hiragana and katakana, even if they are simple: わたしはコーヒーをのみます ("I drink coffee"). The act of writing these sentences, however elementary, reinforces reading and recall simultaneously. Over time, the characters stop being strangers and become trusted companions, guiding you through the landscape of Japanese.

It is also worth noting that mastery of hiragana and katakana carries a symbolic weight beyond utility. They represent your initiation into the language, the moment when you stop being an outsider looking through the glass and step inside. Many learners give up before crossing this threshold, overwhelmed by the belief that Japanese writing is impossibly complex. Yet those who persist discover the opposite: once hiragana and katakana are mastered, the complexity of Japanese begins to simplify. Grammar explanations make sense. Textbook exercises become accessible. Even kanji, daunting as they are, feel more approachable when framed by the phonetic scaffolding of kana.

There is a psychological victory here as well. Every character you master is a tangible achievement. The leap from zero to ninety-two is measurable, visible, and deeply motivating. Unlike the abstract progress of "getting better" at speaking or listening, the concrete act of learning hiragana and katakana gives you proof of your advancement. You can look at a page that once seemed incomprehensible and suddenly read it aloud. That moment of recognition, the spark of understanding, fuels the determination to keep going.

Some learners try to bypass kana by relying on romanization systems like rōmaji, where Japanese words are written in Latin letters. While useful for absolute beginners, rōmaji quickly becomes a crutch. It distances you from the true structure of the language and creates confusion with pronunciation. The sooner you move beyond it, the sooner you step into authentic Japanese. Hiragana and katakana are not obstacles but gateways, and by embracing them early, you align yourself with the rhythm of the language itself.

Learning these first ninety-two characters is not about memorization alone—it is about identity. By mastering hiragana and katakana, you declare to yourself and to the language: *I belong here.* You have taken the first keys, placed them in the lock, and opened the door to everything that follows. Kanji, grammar, conversation—all of it becomes possible because you dared to cross this threshold.

The journey ahead is still long, but with hiragana and katakana at your command, you are no longer standing outside the gates. You are inside the city, navigating its streets, recognizing its signs, and beginning to speak its voice. These two syllabaries are your foundation, your anchor, your compass. They are proof that Japanese, for all its mystique, is a code that can be cracked. And you, step by step, are becoming the codebreaker.

## 2.2 Kanji: From Intimidation to Fascination

For many learners, kanji is the point where enthusiasm meets fear. Hiragana and katakana may feel manageable, but the sheer number of kanji characters—tens of thousands in existence, thousands used daily—creates an impression of an insurmountable wall. Students often approach them with dread, convinced that mastery lies beyond their reach. Yet kanji, once understood not as isolated puzzles but as an interconnected system, transforms from a source of intimidation into a source of fascination.

At the core of this transformation is the radical system. Each kanji is not a random collection of strokes but a composition built from a set of 214 foundational elements known as radicals. These radicals function like the LEGO bricks of the writing system. Alone, they may have simple meanings—tree, water, mouth, person—but combined in different arrangements, they form complex characters. By learning radicals, you gain pattern recognition skills that allow you to decode characters rather than memorize them blindly.

Take, for instance, the radical 木, meaning "tree." When placed next to another 木, it becomes 林, a grove. Add yet another, and it becomes 森, a forest. Suddenly, what seemed like three separate characters reveals itself as a logical progression, each expansion amplifying the concept. This recognition not only simplifies memorization but also makes learning kanji intellectually satisfying. You are not just cramming symbols; you are discovering how Japanese speakers visually represent the world.

This brings us to one of the most effective mnemonic strategies: storytelling. James Heisig's method, famous among Japanese learners, emphasizes creating personal narratives for each kanji, tying its meaning to its components. The genius of this approach is that it taps into the brain's natural ability to remember stories better than abstract data. Consider the character 休, which means "to rest." On the left is the radical for person, 人, and on the right is the radical for tree, 木. By imagining a person leaning against a tree to take a break, you anchor the concept in a vivid image. When you later encounter the character, the story resurfaces effortlessly.

The Heisig method is not about memorizing official definitions but about forging connections that are meaningful to you. If the character 明 (bright) contains the radicals for sun and moon, you might imagine the brilliance when both celestial bodies light the sky. If the character 信 (trust) combines person and word, you might picture someone whose words you can rely on. These images need not be elegant or logical; they only need to be memorable. Over time, your mental library of stories becomes a map through the forest of kanji.

Technology has amplified these strategies with digital tools that turn kanji learning into a game. Platforms like WaniKani employ spaced repetition systems (SRS) to present characters at intervals scientifically proven to optimize memory retention. Each time you recall a character correctly, the interval before it reappears lengthens, ensuring it moves from short-term to long-term memory. Get it wrong, and the system shortens the interval, reinforcing the character until it sticks. This algorithm takes the guesswork out of review, freeing you to focus on learning rather than scheduling.

Other tools like Kanji Garden provide visual maps of progression, showing how characters you know connect to those you are about to learn. Handwriting apps guide you stroke by stroke, ensuring accuracy and helping you develop the muscle memory needed for fluid writing. Each of these digital companions adds a layer of engagement, turning what once felt like rote memorization into an interactive experience.

The shift from intimidation to fascination lies in perspective. If you view kanji as an endless list of arbitrary symbols, discouragement is inevitable. If you view them as a system of building blocks, stories, and patterns, they become a puzzle waiting to be solved. Every character mastered is not just another checkmark—it is a discovery, a glimpse into how language and culture intertwine. The fear that once paralyzed you gives way to curiosity, and kanji ceases to be a wall. It becomes a landscape you are eager to explore.

## 2.3 Reading Real Japanese: Strategic Text Decoding

Learning to read Japanese is not simply about deciphering individual characters or words—it is about developing strategies for handling authentic texts. Too often, learners become trapped in a cycle of painstakingly translating every line, reducing reading to a chore. Others swing to the opposite extreme, skimming over words they do not understand, losing comprehension in the process. The key is balance: knowing when to read intensively and when to read extensively.

Intensive reading involves slowing down, consulting dictionaries, and dissecting grammar in detail. This method is indispensable for building accuracy, especially in the early stages. By working through short passages with care, you develop precision and deepen your understanding of structure. Yet if you rely only on intensive reading, progress feels glacial, and motivation wanes. That is where extensive reading enters. Here, the goal is flow rather than perfection. You read longer passages—graded readers, children's books, or manga—without stopping for every unknown word, trusting that context will fill the gaps. The combination of these approaches trains both accuracy and fluency, much like alternating between weightlifting and running in physical training.

Furigana provides a crucial scaffold in this process. These small hiragana printed above or beside kanji indicate pronunciation, allowing you to focus on comprehension rather than stumbling over unknown characters. Children's books make heavy use of furigana, making them excellent entry points for learners. As you progress, you can transition to young adult novels, where furigana appears less frequently but still supports rare or complex kanji. Eventually, you will encounter newspapers or novels with little to no furigana, by which time your foundation will be strong enough to stand on its own. This graduated exposure mirrors how Japanese children themselves learn, moving from heavy reliance on furigana to confident independence.

Another highly effective method is parallel text reading. In this approach, you use materials where Japanese text is presented alongside an English translation. Bilingual manga, NHK Easy News articles paired with English summaries, and specialized graded readers all provide opportunities to build speed without sacrificing comprehension. When you encounter a difficult phrase, the translation is there to guide you, but the Japanese remains the focus. Over time, the reliance on translation diminishes, and your brain begins to parse meaning directly in Japanese.

This strategy also addresses one of the most common frustrations learners face: the feeling of never knowing enough vocabulary. By encountering words repeatedly in context, rather than memorizing them in isolation, you develop a natural sense of usage. You begin to recognize collocations, idioms, and the rhythm of sentences, all of which resist memorization in lists. Reading in this way transforms vocabulary from static entries in a notebook into living elements of communication.

Equally important is the emotional shift that comes from reading real Japanese. The first time you understand a joke in a manga panel without glancing at the translation, the first time you follow the plot of a children's story unaided, the first time you scan a headline and grasp its meaning—each of these moments provides a surge of confidence. They remind you that Japanese is not confined to drills and exercises; it is a living language, carrying humor, drama, and meaning. These moments accumulate into momentum, turning reading from an obligation into a joy.

Strategic text decoding does not mean perfection. It means equipping yourself with the tools to approach Japanese texts at your current level while steadily pushing into higher ones. With the balance of intensive and extensive reading, the support of furigana, and the guidance of parallel texts, you build a staircase into the world of Japanese literacy. Each page read, however imperfectly, raises you another step. And as the pages multiply, you find that the once-daunting script begins to flow, not as a code to be cracked, but as a voice you can finally hear and understand.

# Chapter 3: Sound Like a Native – Mastering Japanese Pronunciation and Intonation

*"Japanese has only 46 basic sounds compared to English's 44, but pitch accent patterns in Japanese can completely change word meanings – 橋 (bridge) vs. 箸 (chopsticks)."*

## 3.1 The Five Vowel Foundation and Consonant Combinations

When most people begin learning Japanese, they quickly realize that the sounds of the language seem deceptively simple. There are fewer than fifty distinct syllables at the core of the system, and compared to the sprawling array of consonant clusters in English, Japanese syllables appear refreshingly straightforward. Yet, within this apparent simplicity lies a precision that demands care. A single vowel held slightly too long, a consonant doubled instead of spoken once, or a subtle shift in tongue placement can entirely change a word's meaning. Mastering these foundations is not just a matter of accuracy—it is the difference between being understood and causing confusion.

The backbone of Japanese pronunciation is the set of five vowels: あ (a), い (i), う (u), え (e), お (o). While they may look familiar, each carries a crisp, pure sound that does not bend or blur as English vowels often do. English speakers tend to slide between sounds, producing diphthongs without even realizing it. For example, the word "go" in English does not end on a pure "o" but on a blend that drifts toward "u." Japanese vowels, by contrast, remain constant from beginning to end. The "a" in あ is an open sound, steady and unchanging. The "i" in い is sharp and narrow. The "u" in う is produced with rounded lips but without the deep resonance of its English counterpart. To train your mouth to produce these precise vowels, mirror practice becomes indispensable.

By watching your mouth as you pronounce each sound, you learn to identify unnecessary movements and correct them. The jaw drops naturally for あ, while the lips barely move for い. For う, the lips round slightly, but the sound stays forward rather than drifting backward into the throat. え requires a relaxed, open shape, while お closes the lips firmly but not tightly. Practicing in front of a mirror helps you develop awareness, eliminating the unconscious habits carried over from English. Over time, your muscles adjust, and the vowels emerge with the clarity that marks authentic Japanese speech.

Once the vowels are secure, the next challenge is mastering consonant combinations. Unlike English, which permits heavy clusters like "strengths" or "splurge," Japanese restricts syllables to simpler forms: a consonant followed by a vowel, or a single vowel alone. This structure creates a rhythmic, staccato flow, with each syllable occupying nearly the same duration. It also means that every consonant is tethered to a vowel. English learners often struggle with this, attempting to pronounce "desk" as it is in English rather than adapting it into Japanese as デスク (desuku). By learning to hear and produce consonant-vowel pairs as indivisible units, you begin to inhabit the rhythm of Japanese speech.

Perhaps the most notorious sound for English speakers is the Japanese "r," represented in the series ら, り, る, れ, ろ. It is neither the hard, rolling "r" of Spanish nor the liquid "r" of

English. Instead, it is an alveolar tap, produced by flicking the tongue briefly against the ridge just behind the upper teeth. The result lands somewhere between an English "r" and "l," but neither description captures it perfectly. To train this sound, learners can start by producing the sound of a single flap in the American English pronunciation of "butter" when spoken quickly. That light tap, brief and clean, mirrors the Japanese "r."

At first, the alveolar tap may feel unnatural. Your tongue may linger too long or fail to make full contact, producing a muddled sound. But with deliberate practice, the movement becomes second nature. Reading aloud words like *ramen*, *rikai* (understanding), or *rokugatsu* (June) while focusing on the tongue's flick helps solidify the motion. Over time, you discover that the sound is not only achievable but elegant, lending Japanese speech its distinctive smoothness. Conquering this sound is a milestone, marking the moment when your speech begins to shift from foreign approximation to authentic rhythm.

Timing is another critical element of Japanese pronunciation, especially when it comes to double consonants and long vowels. In English, lengthening a vowel often changes emphasis but rarely changes meaning. In Japanese, it creates entirely new words. *Ojisan* (おじさん) means uncle or middle-aged man, while *ojiisan* (おじいさん), with a long "i," means grandfather. Likewise, *biru* (ビル) is building, while *bīru* (ビール) is beer. The difference is subtle but vital.

Double consonants, known as gemination, function similarly. In Japanese, a small つ placed before a consonant indicates a pause or a held sound. For example, *kite* (きて) means "come," while *kitte* (きって), with a doubled "t," means stamp. The meaning hinges on a fraction of a second's difference. To internalize this rhythm, learners often benefit from physical techniques. Some teachers encourage using hand gestures, clapping once for short vowels and twice for long ones, or holding a beat with the palm when encountering double consonants. Others recommend tapping a rhythm on a desk while speaking, aligning syllables with the steady beat and pausing appropriately for gemination. These exercises transform abstract timing into a physical sensation, embedding the rhythm into muscle memory.

The importance of these distinctions cannot be overstated. A misplaced vowel length or overlooked double consonant may not always derail comprehension, but it will mark your speech as foreign and occasionally cause misunderstandings. By practicing with deliberate attention, you develop sensitivity to timing, gradually internalizing it until it becomes instinctive. Eventually, you no longer need to think consciously about holding a vowel or pausing before a consonant; your speech flows naturally within the framework of Japanese rhythm.

It is worth emphasizing that Japanese pronunciation is not about theatrical imitation but about precision and restraint. Unlike English, which often rewards dramatic intonation, Japanese values subtlety. Each syllable is clear, each vowel stable, each consonant consistent. The artistry lies not in embellishment but in consistency. Once you align your speech with these principles, you begin to sound not like someone struggling to reproduce foreign sounds but like someone moving comfortably within the language itself.

This foundation of vowels, consonant combinations, and rhythm is more than mechanical training. It is the gateway to deeper levels of communication. When you pronounce words with clarity, listeners focus on your message rather than your accent. When you respect the timing of long vowels and double consonants, you demonstrate not only skill but cultural sensitivity, showing that you take the language seriously. And when you conquer the elusive "r," you give yourself the gift of authenticity, a sound that resonates with the cadence of Japanese itself.

Above all, these elements remind you that sounding native is not about perfection but about integration. Each time you adjust your vowels, refine your consonants, and practice your timing, you are aligning your voice with the music of Japanese. Slowly, steadily, your speech ceases to be translation and becomes expression. The five vowels are no longer foreign—they are part of your own voice. The consonant-vowel pairs become second nature. The alveolar tap ceases to be a trick and becomes a habit. And the rhythm of long and short sounds weaves itself into your sentences until your words, once hesitant, flow with confidence.

Mastering Japanese pronunciation begins here, with the foundation of vowels and consonants. It may seem simple, even childlike, compared to the complex structures of grammar or the vast landscape of kanji. Yet it is here, in these smallest of sounds, that the soul of the language resides. To speak Japanese authentically, you must first honor its building blocks. Once you do, every word you utter carries not only meaning but the unmistakable sound of belonging.

## 3.2 Pitch Accent Patterns: The Hidden Melody of Japanese

To the untrained ear, Japanese may sound flat, almost monotone compared to English or Spanish, which rise and fall dramatically in intonation. Yet beneath that surface calm lies a subtle system of pitch that gives the language its melody. This is the realm of pitch accent, a feature that, once ignored, can turn words into riddles, but once understood, transforms speech into music. Mastering pitch accent is not about singing your sentences; it is about aligning your voice with a rhythm that Japanese listeners subconsciously expect.

Standard Japanese, especially the Tokyo dialect, organizes words into four fundamental pitch patterns: flat, rising, falling, and rise-fall. Each pattern shifts the meaning of a word not by changing vowels or consonants but by altering the pitch assigned to syllables. Consider the pair 橋 (hashi, bridge) and 箸 (hashi, chopsticks). To an English speaker, they sound identical, but to a Japanese ear, they are as different as "cat" and "cut." One begins with a high pitch that drops, while the other remains steady. Mastering these contrasts is not an optional flourish; it is central to being understood.

Flat patterns keep the voice steady, with no rise or fall across the syllables. Rising patterns begin low and climb higher, creating a gentle upward slope. Falling patterns start high and then descend, signaling the end of emphasis. The rise-fall pattern, more complex, climbs early and then drops before the word finishes, producing a wave-like contour. Each type carries dozens of examples, and practicing them side by side sharpens your ear. Reading minimal pairs aloud—words distinguished only by pitch—trains you to hear and reproduce the hidden melody.

Awareness of pitch accent also means recognizing its regional variations. The Tokyo standard, taught in most classrooms, is only one flavor of Japanese. In Osaka and other parts of Kansai, the melody changes. Words that fall in Tokyo rise in Osaka; sentences delivered flat in Tokyo may dance with greater intonation in Kansai. These differences are not just academic curiosities. They carry social meaning. A Tokyo pitch in Osaka may sound stiff or overly formal, while an Osaka pitch in Tokyo may sound casual or comedic. For learners aiming to use Japanese in professional contexts, aligning with Tokyo patterns offers neutrality and wide recognition. For those cultivating friendships or engaging with regional media, sensitivity to dialectal pitch adds richness to communication.

Training pitch is not accomplished by reading charts alone. It requires living sound, and one of the most effective techniques is shadowing. This involves listening to authentic Japanese—drama dialogue, newscasts, or TV shows—and speaking simultaneously with the actors, mimicking their rhythm, pitch, and timing. At first, shadowing feels overwhelming, like trying to sing along to a song in a language you barely know. But with persistence, your voice begins to follow the contour naturally. The muscles of your throat and tongue adapt, and your ear grows accustomed to subtle rises and falls. Over time, shadowing builds an instinctive sense of pitch that no textbook can provide.

Japanese dramas are particularly effective tools because they showcase a range of contexts. Business scenes display formal, restrained pitch; family conversations reveal casual warmth; comedic moments exaggerate intonation for effect. By shadowing across genres, you expose yourself to the spectrum of pitch usage. This immersion not only improves pronunciation but also deepens cultural understanding. You come to see pitch not merely as a technical hurdle but as a living aspect of expression, shaping how sincerity, authority, or humor is conveyed.

Pitch accent may never feel as natural to a learner as it does to a native, but with training, it becomes second nature enough to avoid misunderstandings. More importantly, it makes your Japanese resonate as authentic rather than foreign. To a Japanese listener, the difference is immediate, subtle, and powerful: your words do not float awkwardly but land with the cadence of their language's melody.

## 3.3 Conversational Flow and Natural Expressions

If pitch accent gives Japanese its melody, conversational flow gives it its soul. Many learners can construct grammatically correct sentences, yet their speech feels stiff, robotic, or distant. What separates learners from natives is not the mastery of textbook phrases but the mastery of rhythm, fillers, and the invisible signals that make conversation alive. This is where aizuchi, sentence-final particles, and the concept of 間 (ma, pause) come into play.

Aizuchi refers to the small, frequent sounds Japanese speakers use to show they are listening: そうですね ("yes, indeed"), なるほど ("I see"), ええ ("uh-huh"). Unlike in English, where backchanneling may occur sporadically, in Japanese it is expected and constant. Silence while listening can feel disinterested or even rude. By sprinkling aizuchi throughout a conversation, you show engagement, respect, and alignment with the speaker. Mastering aizuchi is not difficult, but it requires practice to insert them naturally, without interrupting. At first, you may overuse them or place them awkwardly. With time, you learn to drop them in at the right moments, nodding along and creating the rhythm of real dialogue.

Equally important are the sentence-final particles, tiny words that carry emotional weight far beyond their size. Take ね, often translated as "isn't it?" but in practice serving to seek confirmation, invite agreement, or soften statements. Compare it to よ, which asserts certainty or gives information with confidence. A simple sentence like 行く ("I go") changes tone dramatically when you add these particles: 行くね ("I'm going, okay?"), 行くよ ("I'm going, you know"), 行くわ (a softer, often feminine nuance), 行くぞ (a masculine, assertive edge), or 行くさ (a casual, slightly rebellious tone). Each particle shades the sentence with emotion, turning bare information into communication colored by relationship and intent.

For learners, these particles are both challenging and liberating. They are challenging because their usage defies direct translation. They cannot be memorized as equivalents of English phrases but must be felt in context. Yet they are liberating because they give you tools to express personality, warmth, and subtlety in Japanese. Without them, your sentences may be correct but lifeless. With them, your speech begins to breathe.

Underlying all this is the Japanese appreciation of 間 (ma), the meaningful pause. In Western communication, silence often signals discomfort or the need to fill space. In Japanese, silence can signal thoughtfulness, respect, or emphasis. A well-timed pause can carry more weight than a string of words. It allows the listener to reflect, the speaker to show restraint, and the conversation to flow without pressure. Learning to use ma requires sensitivity. You must resist the urge to rush, to fill every gap, and instead allow silence to play its part in the music of speech.

The interplay of aizuchi, particles, and ma creates a conversational texture unique to Japanese. Imagine a dialogue where one speaker shares an idea, the other responds with なるほど, a pause follows, then a gentle ね to invite further thoughts. The exchange is not a battle of words but a dance, where each move acknowledges and complements the other. For a learner, stepping into this dance means moving beyond translation and into cultural rhythm.

To practice, immerse yourself in real conversations through media or language partners. Listen not only to what is said but to how it is said—the constant backchanneling, the softening particles, the pauses that punctuate thought. Mimic these patterns, even in your own practice. Record yourself speaking and insert aizuchi as if you were listening to another. Pause deliberately, letting the silence linger. Add particles to your sentences and feel the shift in tone. Gradually, your speech will lose its rigidity and take on the flow of natural Japanese.

This mastery of flow is not about sounding perfect. It is about sounding alive, about making your Japanese not a series of dictionary entries strung together but a conversation that breathes with the rhythm of the culture. When you reach this stage, you no longer feel like an outsider assembling sentences. You feel like a participant in the shared art of communication, where words, pauses, and tones intertwine.

# Chapter 4: Grammar That Sticks – Building Sentences Like a Japanese Architect

*"While English follows Subject-Verb-Object, Japanese's Subject-Object-Verb structure mirrors 45% of world languages, making it a gateway to learning Korean, Turkish, and Hindi."*

## 4.1 The Particle System: Your Sentence GPS

Every learner of Japanese eventually comes face to face with particles, those small but mighty markers that appear between words and seem to defy direct translation. To a newcomer, they can feel like confusing fragments scattered across sentences without clear purpose. To a native speaker, however, they are the glue that holds meaning together, the compass points that orient every statement. Without particles, Japanese would collapse into ambiguity; with them, sentences unfold with precision, elegance, and flow. Understanding them is like learning to navigate a vast city: once you know the train lines and stations, the entire map becomes coherent.

In English, relationships between words are usually defined by strict word order. "The cat chased the dog" differs entirely from "The dog chased the cat," because position dictates who acts and who receives the action. Japanese, by contrast, relies on particles rather than position. Because verbs always come at the end, particles function as the markers that reveal roles within the sentence. Think of them as signposts or station names on a railway line. Each noun boards the train, but its particle specifies where it's headed and how it connects to the rest of the journey.

Consider the particle は, often introduced as the "topic marker." It signals what the sentence is about, placing emphasis not on the subject as in English but on the broader frame of reference. If you say 私は学生です, you are stating, "As for me, I am a student." The particle は orients the listener, much like the opening of a map that shows which city you're in before you trace the roads. Contrast this with が, frequently labeled as the "subject marker." While は sets the stage, が highlights what stands out or carries emphasis in that particular moment. If someone asks who is eating the cake and you reply ケーキを食べているのは私が, you are shining a light on yourself, marking yourself as the subject of focus.

Then there is を, which designates the direct object. In English, objects fall naturally after the verb—"eat cake," "see the mountain." But in Japanese, the verb waits at the end, so the particle を must signal the object early. ケーキを食べる leaves no doubt: cake is what is eaten. Without を, the sentence loses its anchor, leaving the listener adrift.

Other particles map out directions, places, and relationships. に signals destination, marking where something is headed. 日本に行く means "to go to Japan," the に functioning as the destination station. Confuse it with で, however, and the meaning shifts entirely. 日本で行く suggests not going to Japan but going somewhere while in Japan, the emphasis moving from destination to location of action. One particle, a single syllable, transforms the meaning completely.

Particle と serves as the connector, binding nouns together like carriages in a train. ケーキとコーヒー means "cake and coffee." But と also marks companionship: 友達と行く is "to go with a friend." The particle から introduces origins, both physical and temporal. 学校から帰る means "to return from school." Meanwhile, まで defines limits or endpoints, as in 駅まで歩く, "to walk as far as the station." Together, these core particles create the basic network of Japanese grammar, mapping out who acts, what is acted upon, where, how, and with whom.

Yet the real fascination emerges when particles combine or layer, producing nuanced meanings. Take には, which blends に with は. While に alone points to a destination or point in time, には adds emphasis, framing the destination as the topic. 日本には美しい山が多い shifts the nuance from "going to Japan" to "as for Japan, it has many beautiful mountains." Similarly, では merges で with は, turning location into the frame of focus: 東京では物価が高い highlights that specifically in Tokyo, prices are high. These combinations reflect the way particles don't merely glue words together but sculpt the contours of thought, emphasizing contrasts, drawing attention, and shaping context.

The particle との brings subtlety when linking ideas. While と simply means "with" or "and," adding の turns the connection into a possessive or descriptive relationship. 友達との会話 refers to a "conversation with a friend," but it carries a more formal or literary nuance, elevating the relationship beyond casual mention. Likewise, からの can express origin in more layered contexts. 大阪からの手紙 is not just "a letter from Osaka" but carries a sense of directionality and origin embedded in the phrasing, making the source part of the identity of the object.

These subtleties explain why particles challenge learners so deeply: they resist one-to-one translation and instead demand an understanding of relationships. Each particle is not a fixed English equivalent but a tool that shapes meaning based on placement, emphasis, and combination. Mastering them means thinking less in terms of "What does this particle mean?" and more in terms of "What relationship is this particle creating here?"

Mistakes with particles are common, and sometimes they alter meaning so drastically that sentences shift into unintended territory. Take the earlier example of 日本に行く versus 日本で行く. The first expresses going to Japan, a journey across borders. The second implies performing the act of going somewhere while inside Japan. To an English speaker, the difference seems minor, but to a Japanese listener, the nuance is critical. Similarly, confusing が and は can warp the intended focus. If someone asks who did the homework and you reply with 私はしました rather than 私がしました, you might be interpreted as stating a fact about yourself rather than directly answering the question.

These distinctions matter not only for correctness but for connection. Japanese relies heavily on context, and particles serve as the subtle threads weaving context together. When you use them accurately, your sentences resonate with clarity and precision, allowing conversations to flow smoothly. When misused, they create small but noticeable snags, moments of confusion that remind the listener you are still on the outside of the linguistic system.

The good news is that particles, though challenging, respond well to visualization and practice. Picture each sentence as a train line, with particles as the stations that mark changes in direction, origin, or emphasis. Without stations, a train becomes disoriented; without particles, a sentence loses coherence. By training yourself to see these stations, you move from stringing words together to navigating meaning deliberately.

Over time, as you grow more comfortable, particles cease to feel like foreign symbols needing translation. They become intuitive markers guiding the flow of your thoughts. You no longer pause to ask, "Should it be に or で?"—you simply feel the direction the sentence is taking and choose accordingly. This shift is the essence of mastery: when grammar stops being rules to remember and becomes the natural architecture of expression.

Particles are not the enemy of the learner. They are the language's navigational system, subtle yet indispensable, ensuring every sentence reaches its destination. To embrace them is to accept the way Japanese structures meaning: not through rigid word order, but through delicate markers that orient thought. With patience, practice, and awareness, the particle system transforms from a maze into a map, guiding you not only through Japanese grammar but through the very mindset of its speakers.

## 4.2 Verb Conjugation: The Swiss Army Knife of Japanese

If particles are the rails that guide a Japanese sentence, verbs are the engines that drive it forward. Without them, nothing moves, nothing happens. But unlike English verbs, which rely on auxiliary words and often irregular patterns, Japanese verbs carry immense flexibility within themselves. A single stem can expand into dozens of forms, unlocking shades of meaning from respect and humility to causation and possibility. For learners, this is daunting at first, but once the patterns click, verbs reveal themselves as one of the most powerful and versatile aspects of the language.

The foundation begins with the recognition that Japanese verbs fall into three categories: Group 1 (godan), Group 2 (ichidan), and a small set of irregulars. Godan verbs, also called consonant-stem verbs, shift their final consonant depending on the conjugation. Take 書く, "to write." Its stem, kaku, transforms smoothly: 書きます in polite form, 書いた in past tense, 書ける in potential form. The endings change like gears, but the engine remains steady. Ichidan verbs, often ending in る with an -e or -i vowel sound, are even more predictable. 食べる, "to eat," becomes 食べます, 食べた, 食べられる. Their stems remain intact, shedding or adding only the る as needed. Then there are the irregulars, notably する and 来る, whose unique patterns must be memorized but occur so frequently that they become second nature.

The challenge is not just memorizing forms but internalizing them until recognition becomes reflex. Creating charts, reciting patterns, and writing practice sentences help, but the real breakthrough comes when you start seeing verbs not as isolated units but as families. Once you learn how 書く conjugates, you can apply the same template to 聞く, 行く, 泳ぐ, and countless others. The patterns replicate, creating a sense of rhythm. Instead of facing thousands of separate words, you face only a handful of patterns, each multiplied across verbs like a formula applied in mathematics.

At the center of this system sits the て-form, often called the heart of Japanese verbs. With it, you unlock a vast array of structures, each building on the same simple base. Want to make a request? Add ください: 書いてください, "please write." Want to express ongoing action? Use いる: 書いている, "is writing." Want to connect clauses? Stack them: 本を読んで、寝ました, "I read a book and then slept." The て-form extends further into giving permission, describing experiences, or linking reasons. With one form, you gain access to over twenty grammatical functions, each unfolding naturally once you master the rhythm.

But verbs also carry the weight of politeness, a central axis of Japanese communication. Where English toggles between formal and informal mainly through vocabulary choices or tone, Japanese codifies politeness into its verb forms. At the basic level, you distinguish between plain form—書く, 食べる, 行く—and polite form—書きます, 食べます, 行きます. Yet the spectrum extends much further. 敬語, or honorific language, subdivides into 尊敬語 (respectful language), where the speaker elevates the listener or subject, and 謙譲語 (humble language), where the speaker lowers themselves to show deference. Thus 行く becomes いらっしゃる in respect and 参る in humility, depending on the relationship between speaker, listener, and subject.

Navigating these levels can feel like learning multiple parallel languages, but they reflect the architecture of Japanese society. Conversations in a business meeting, among friends, and within family all demand different registers. Using the wrong form risks sounding rude, arrogant, or awkward. Mastery does not mean switching perfectly from day one but developing sensitivity to context, listening carefully to how others address you, and gradually adapting. At the opposite end of the spectrum lies タメ口, the casual register of close friends, where contractions, plain forms, and playful tones dominate. Moving between these layers is like shifting gears in a finely tuned vehicle, allowing you to adapt to terrain and company with fluidity.

Verb conjugation, then, is less a set of burdensome rules than a Swiss army knife. Once you know how to unfold its blades, you realize that nearly every communicative need—respect, humility, causation, continuity, possibility—emerges from the same compact structure. The journey from bewilderment to mastery mirrors the journey of learning Japanese itself: what seems overwhelming at first condenses into elegance once the patterns reveal themselves.

## 4.3 Sentence Architecture: From Simple to Sophisticated

While verbs provide the action and particles lay the track, the architecture of Japanese sentences emerges most clearly in how ideas are layered. A beginner starts with simple declaratives: 私は学生です, "I am a student." But Japanese allows, even encourages, complexity through modifier stacking, cause-and-effect structures, and indirect communication. These techniques build sentences that not only convey facts but reflect the subtleties of thought and culture.

Modifier stacking is perhaps the most striking feature. In English, modifiers usually precede or follow nouns directly: "the red book," "the book that I bought yesterday." Japanese builds such modifications backwards, placing descriptive clauses before the noun they qualify. 昨日買った本 is literally "yesterday bought book," compacting an entire relative clause into a phrase. Layering continues indefinitely: 公園で遊んでいる子供たちの笑顔, "the smiles of the children playing in the park." Each modifier slots in front of the noun, stacking detail upon detail until a vivid picture emerges. At first, this backward construction feels disorienting, but once mastered, it becomes a powerful tool for compressing information into elegant units.

Cause-and-effect relationships extend this architecture, with particles and phrases shaping the degree of formality. から is straightforward and often used in casual speech: 疲れたから寝る, "I'm going to sleep because I'm tired." ので softens the tone, suitable for polite contexts: 疲れたので寝ます. The particle し allows for multiple reasons: 暑いし、疲れたし、出かけたくない, "It's hot, and I'm tired, so I don't want to go out." For more formal writing or explanations, ために introduces purpose or reason, as in 勉強するために図書館へ

行く, "I go to the library in order to study." Each structure provides not just logical connection but social calibration, signaling how directly or gently you assert your reasoning.

Perhaps most characteristic of Japanese communication, however, is the art of indirectness. Whereas English often values clarity through direct assertion, Japanese often prefers subtlety, allowing room for interpretation and harmony. Grammar itself provides the tools. Passive voice shifts focus away from the agent: ドアが開けられた avoids naming who opened the door, leaving the act itself in focus. Potential forms emphasize possibility rather than blunt capability: 日本語が話せる softens "I speak Japanese" into "I am able to speak Japanese." Provisional statements further blur certainty, offering conditional frameworks: 雨が降れば行きません, "If it rains, I won't go." These structures allow speakers to present ideas in ways that soften disagreement, avoid confrontation, or respect ambiguity.

Understanding this indirect style is not just a matter of grammar but of cultural insight. In Japan, relationships are preserved by leaving space for nuance. A blunt "no" may give way to expressions like ちょっと難しいですね, "that seems a little difficult," where grammar carries politeness through understatement. To master Japanese sentences, therefore, is to master not only structures but intentions: the ability to convey meaning without closing doors.

The evolution from simple to sophisticated sentences is not instantaneous. It begins with particles and verbs, then grows into stacked modifiers, causal chains, and nuanced forms of indirectness. Each step reflects both linguistic mechanics and cultural philosophy. English builds complexity by adding clauses and conjunctions; Japanese builds it by layering and softening, creating sentences that often resemble carefully crafted architecture.

When you learn to think this way, you begin to design your sentences like a Japanese architect designs a house: with balance, flow, and sensitivity to the environment. Details are arranged not randomly but in deliberate order. Spaces are left intentionally, pauses respected, indirect angles introduced where direct lines might disrupt harmony. Grammar ceases to be rules written in textbooks and becomes a living design, shaping how you construct and inhabit ideas.

# Chapter 5: Words That Work – Strategic Vocabulary Acquisition

*"Research shows that knowing just 1,000 Japanese words covers 75% of daily conversation, while 2,000 words unlock 80% of written texts."*

## 5.1 Core Vocabulary: The Essential 2,000

When learners imagine mastering Japanese vocabulary, they often picture memorizing endless lists, stacks of flashcards, and nights spent drilling isolated words until exhaustion sets in. This fear, more than anything else, discourages people from pursuing Japanese seriously. But vocabulary acquisition does not need to be an endless uphill struggle. It can be approached strategically, with attention to frequency, themes, and patterns. By focusing on the most common and useful words, grouping them in meaningful ways, and leveraging the history and structure of the language itself, you can build a foundation that supports fluent communication far faster than brute force memorization ever could.

The reality is simple but powerful: not all words are created equal. Japanese, like every language, follows patterns of frequency. Some words appear constantly in daily speech and writing, while others lurk at the margins, surfacing only in academic texts or poetic contexts. Research from the Balanced Corpus of Contemporary Written Japanese (BCCWJ) demonstrates that a relatively small number of words account for the majority of language use. Just one thousand words cover three-quarters of everyday spoken interactions. Two thousand extend that coverage to the vast majority of newspapers, novels, and online writing. Beyond that, gains become incremental. The lesson is clear: aim first for the core vocabulary that truly powers communication.

This frequency-based approach shifts the mindset from quantity to quality. Instead of scattering your energy across obscure or flashy words, you target the statistical backbone of the language. The result is immediate payoff. Within months, you find yourself recognizing words in conversations, signs, or dramas that recur again and again, reinforcing themselves through context. Each encounter strengthens memory, turning passive recognition into active recall. The first two thousand words are not just a starting point; they are the keys that open most doors you will encounter in Japanese life.

But even within this core, the method of organization matters. Traditional textbooks often present vocabulary in alphabetical order or as random sets detached from context. The learner dutifully repeats: "apple, dog, table, blue," without any sense of when these words might arise together in real conversation. A more effective strategy is thematic clustering. This involves grouping words by situations you are likely to experience—shopping, work, travel, dining, leisure—so that each cluster forms a coherent mental map. Imagine learning the words for "buy," "sell," "price," "shop," and "cash" as a cluster. When you step into a Japanese store, those words surface together, ready for use. Contrast that with trying to recall "buy" from one chapter, "cash" from another, and "price" from yet another. Clustering accelerates acquisition by mirroring the way words naturally appear in life.

Thematic grouping also creates emotional connection. Words tied to experiences carry more weight than abstract entries. If you love cooking, learning 食べる (to eat), 飲む (to drink), 料理 (cooking), and 味 (flavor) as a family resonates more deeply than rote lists. When you cook dinner and narrate your actions in Japanese, the vocabulary sticks because it is embedded in lived activity. Similarly, travelers preparing for Japan find motivation in mastering terms like 電車 (train), 切符 (ticket), and 乗り換え (transfer), which immediately empower them in real contexts. Vocabulary ceases to be sterile data and becomes a living tool.

Beyond frequency and themes lies another powerful advantage: etymology. Japanese vocabulary draws heavily from two sources—native Japanese words (kun-yomi) and Chinese-derived words (on-yomi). Understanding these layers is like discovering hidden word families that multiply your knowledge. For instance, the character 学, associated with learning, appears in 学校 (school), 学生 (student), and 学問 (scholarship). Recognizing this root allows you to decode new words on sight, even before formal study. Similarly, 読 (to read) combines with 書 (to write) in 読書, meaning "reading books." Instead of treating every word as isolated, you see them as branches growing from common roots.

This approach not only accelerates acquisition but deepens appreciation for the language. You begin to see the logic behind Japanese word formation, where combinations of kanji generate nuanced meanings. The contrast between kun-yomi and on-yomi readings further enriches understanding. 山, as kun-yomi, is やま (yama, mountain) in words like 富士山 (Mount Fuji). But its on-yomi reading appears in 火山 (kazan, volcano). One character, multiple readings, each unlocking new contexts. At first, this multiplicity may seem like chaos, but with practice, it reveals itself as a map of cultural history, showing how Japanese evolved by blending native and Chinese influences.

To master vocabulary, therefore, is not to memorize blindly but to build networks. Frequency tells you which words matter most. Thematic clustering embeds them into real-life contexts.

Etymology connects them into families, reducing the burden of memorization. Together, these strategies create a virtuous cycle: words appear often, words connect to your life, and words form patterns. Every encounter reinforces memory, every use strengthens recall, and every discovery adds momentum.

The payoff becomes evident when you read or listen to Japanese media. Instead of feeling lost in a sea of unknown terms, you begin to catch recurring anchors—common verbs, particles, nouns. From these anchors, you infer surrounding meanings, filling gaps with context. Conversations once incomprehensible begin to shimmer with familiarity. You may not understand every detail, but you grasp the core. This is fluency in its early form: not perfection, but functionality.

It is important to note that vocabulary learning thrives on active engagement. Reading words in lists may introduce them, but using them cements them. Speaking them aloud, writing them in sentences, hearing them in podcasts, or spotting them in manga all reinforce retention. Each encounter shifts the word from passive recognition to active command. The goal is not merely to "know" two thousand words but to wield them with confidence, ready to deploy in speech or writing without hesitation.

Learners often wonder how long this process takes. The answer depends less on time than on method. A scattered, unstructured approach may yield little progress in years. A focused, strategic approach, emphasizing frequency, clustering, and patterns, can deliver functional vocabulary within months. The difference lies in alignment: aligning your study with how language actually functions in daily life.

Perhaps the most encouraging truth is this: two thousand words is not an impossible mountain. It is finite, countable, achievable. Unlike the open-ended vastness of "learn Japanese," mastering this core is a tangible goal. And once achieved, it changes everything. With two thousand words, you can read newspapers with support, watch dramas with subtitles and recognize half the dialogue, hold conversations about daily life, and navigate Japan with confidence. You may not yet debate philosophy or read classical poetry, but you are no longer a beginner. You are a participant, engaged and equipped.

Vocabulary, in the end, is not about amassing endless knowledge but about building bridges. Each word is a plank across the river of misunderstanding. Two thousand planks carry you across most of the waters. From there, you can decide whether to expand further into specialized domains, but the essential crossing has been made. Words that once seemed like scattered fragments become tools that work, words that allow you to speak, to listen, to read, and to live in Japanese.

## 5.2 Collocations and Natural Word Partnerships

One of the most underestimated aspects of vocabulary acquisition is the study of collocations, the natural partnerships between words that native speakers use instinctively but learners often overlook. Knowing a word in isolation does not guarantee that you can use it fluently. Fluency depends on using words in combinations that sound natural to the ear of a native speaker. Without this awareness, speech risks sounding awkward even if technically correct.

Japanese offers an especially rich field for collocational study because it relies heavily on certain recurring patterns, particularly with verbs like する. The verb する may appear deceptively simple, often translated as "to do." But in practice, it functions as the foundation for countless expressions. Take 勉強する, to study, or 準備する, to prepare. Add 確認する, to check or confirm, and you already cover three essential actions used in schools, offices, and daily life. By mastering a range of する verbs, you suddenly expand your expressive range without needing to memorize entirely new verb stems. Instead of learning a hundred different action verbs, you can combine nouns with する, unlocking hundreds of ready-made expressions that feel natural to a native speaker.

Collocations also extend into the world of adjective-noun partnerships. In English, certain combinations feel instinctively correct—"strong tea," "heavy rain"—while others, like "powerful tea" or "thick rain," sound strange even though the words themselves make sense. Japanese follows the same principle. 激しい雨, "intense rain," sounds natural, while 強い雨, literally "strong rain," although grammatically valid, lacks the idiomatic feel. For learners, this presents both a challenge and an opportunity. It is not enough to know adjectives and nouns; you must learn the partnerships that carry meaning in real use. Listening to native material, reading authentic texts, and paying attention to these patterns helps develop an ear for natural pairings. Over time, you begin to sense which adjectives fit with which nouns, shifting from mechanical word assembly to authentic expression.

Another dimension of natural word partnerships in Japanese is its extraordinary use of onomatopoeia. Where English employs a handful of sound-symbolic words like "buzz" or "crash," Japanese boasts over 4,000 such expressions, covering not only sounds but feelings, textures, states of being, and even subtle shades of motion. Words like ドキドキ capture the pounding of a heart, ザーザー evokes pouring rain, and キラキラ describes sparkling light. Others, like しとしと, convey the quiet, steady patter of drizzle, distinct from the roar of ザーザー. These expressions add color, intimacy, and vividness to speech, allowing nuance that plain vocabulary cannot achieve.

Mastering onomatopoeia is not about memorizing thousands of forms overnight but about gradually integrating them into your active vocabulary. They enrich descriptions, making them feel alive. Saying 心臓がドキドキしている expresses nervous excitement more vividly than a literal translation like "my heart is beating fast." Children grow up using these words instinctively, and adults weave them into daily conversation, manga, and advertising. By learning them, you not only sound more natural but also gain insight into how Japanese speakers perceive and describe their world.

Together, collocations, adjective-noun partnerships, and onomatopoeic expressions elevate vocabulary from mere correctness to native-like fluency. They transform speech from flat to textured, from understandable to memorable. In the same way a painter uses not just primary colors but blends and shades, a learner who embraces these word partnerships begins to paint with the full palette of Japanese.

## 5.3 Memory Techniques for Long-term Retention

Acquiring vocabulary is only half the battle; the other half is keeping it. Many learners know the frustration of studying a word, recognizing it in an exercise, and then forgetting it days later when it arises in conversation. Retention is not a matter of willpower alone but of method. The brain favors certain types of input, and by aligning study with these natural tendencies, you can move words from fragile short-term storage into durable long-term memory.

One effective approach is the Keyword Method, adapted specifically for Japanese. This technique involves creating mental bridges between Japanese words and concepts you already know, drawing on both sound and meaning. Take the word 雲 (くも), meaning cloud. You might link it to the English word "comb," imagining combing through fluffy clouds. The sillier or more vivid the image, the more likely it will stick. Another example is 鳥 (とり), bird, which you might link to "tori gate," visualizing a bird flying through a shrine gate. The brain remembers images and stories more easily than abstract symbols, so these mnemonic bridges give words a foothold until repeated use makes them natural.

Yet memory also depends on timing. The principle of spaced repetition has transformed vocabulary learning worldwide, and Japanese learners benefit from customizing it to the unique challenges of the language. Systems like Anki, based on spaced repetition, schedule reviews at intervals designed to maximize retention while minimizing effort. See a word too often, and you waste time; see it too rarely, and you forget it. The algorithm fine-tunes exposure to ensure reinforcement just before forgetting occurs. For Japanese, customization means more than adjusting intervals. It involves addressing kanji with multiple readings, ensuring you practice both recognition (reading) and production (writing). It may also mean including pitch accent information, so that you recall not only the meaning of 橋 and 箸 but also the subtle difference in tone that separates bridge from chopsticks.

The most crucial principle, however, is production. Recognition alone is insufficient for fluency. Seeing a word and knowing what it means is passive knowledge; using it in a sentence is active mastery. Studies consistently show that writing words in context or speaking them aloud accelerates retention by up to three times compared to recognition drills alone. This is because production forces deeper processing. To create a sentence, you must retrieve the word, align it with grammar, and pronounce it—all of which reinforce memory more powerfully than passive review.

Practical methods for applying this principle include journaling in Japanese, even if your sentences are simple and imperfect. Writing 今日の天気は暑かった, "today's weather was hot," cements not only the word for weather but also its collocation with "hot." Similarly, speaking aloud during study sessions, narrating your actions, or practicing dialogues out loud pushes words into active use. What you can say, you truly know. What you can only recognize, you risk losing.

Combining these techniques creates a cycle of retention. Mnemonics bring words into memory. Spaced repetition keeps them alive. Production locks them in place through active recall. The learner who employs all three does not merely accumulate vocabulary but builds a durable lexicon that endures.

Retention is also emotional. Words tied to personal experiences stick more firmly than abstract lists. If you learn the word 猫 because you love cats, every encounter with your pet reinforces it. If you learn the word 電車 before a trip to Japan and use it while boarding trains, it embeds itself in memory with far more force than any flashcard. Memory thrives on relevance. The more you tie words to your life, your passions, and your goals, the more permanent they become.

In the end, vocabulary mastery is not about endless repetition but about smart repetition, not about brute memorization but about creative association. By blending keyword mnemonics, optimized review systems, and active production, you create conditions where words flourish in memory. They cease to be fragile entries on a flashcard and become living tools, ready whenever you need them.

# Chapter 6: Real Conversations – From Textbook to Street Japanese

*"70% of actual Japanese conversation uses forms and expressions rarely taught in textbooks, including 2,500+ common abbreviations and colloquialisms."*

## 6.1 Daily Life Interactions: Beyond "How Are You?"

For many learners, the first shock upon arriving in Japan is not the sight of neon-lit streets, temples nestled among skyscrapers, or trains arriving with perfect punctuality. The real surprise is how little of their carefully memorized textbook Japanese seems to prepare them for everyday encounters. You may know how to say "How are you?" in formal Japanese, but you quickly notice that nobody greets each other with お元気ですか outside of polite correspondence or first meetings. Instead, you hear 元気?, 調子どう?, or simply a casual nod. This gap between classroom dialogues and lived conversations is where many students feel stranded, unable to bridge the polished but artificial sentences they studied with the rapid, abbreviated exchanges of real life.

One of the best training grounds for navigating authentic speech is the convenience store—the *conbini*. In a typical visit, you are greeted at lightning speed with いらっしゃいませ, the melodic welcome that pours out as a single unit rather than four distinct words. At the counter, the cashier may fire off a string of questions before you have even placed your items down. ポイントカードはお持ちですか?—do you have a point card? If you hesitate, you may catch only the final ですか, leaving you unsure how to answer. Then comes 袋はご利用ですか?—would you like a bag? Increasingly, stores encourage customers to refuse bags, and the interaction moves so quickly that you need ready responses. A simple はい、お願いします secures a bag, while 大丈夫です declines politely. Payment adds another layer: cash transactions are accompanied by trays for coins, while card payments may trigger the phrase 暗証番号をお願いします, requesting your PIN.

At first, these exchanges feel overwhelming. But the beauty is that the patterns repeat almost identically every time. After a handful of visits, the rhythm becomes predictable. You know what the cashier will ask, in what order, and how to respond. Practicing these set pieces transforms the conbini from a site of anxiety into a rehearsal stage where you refine your listening and speaking reflexes. Unlike free conversation, which can spiral in unpredictable directions, convenience store dialogue is structured, efficient, and repetitive—the perfect environment for learners to sharpen survival Japanese.

Restaurants offer another arena where classroom Japanese often falters. Entering a restaurant in Japan, you are met not with a simple hello but with the resonant いらっしゃいませ. When staff approach your table, they may ask お決まりですか?—literally, "Have you decided?" A learner expecting 何を食べますか? may hesitate, but the intent is clear: they want your order. Responding can be as simple as pointing and saying これをください, yet more natural phrases include お願いします appended to the dish name. Drinks are often requested separately, and confirming orders may involve the staff repeating them back at rapid speed.

The payment ritual carries its own conventions. Staff might ask ご一緒でよろしいですか?, which translates literally to "Is it all together?" They are not questioning your unity but whether you will pay on one bill or separately. Answering はい confirms a single bill, while 別々で indicates separate checks. These phrases rarely appear in beginner textbooks, yet they recur daily in Japanese life. By internalizing them, you not only navigate restaurants smoothly but also gain insight into the cultural rhythm of service interactions, where politeness and efficiency intertwine.

Perhaps the most intimidating realm for learners is the telephone. Unlike face-to-face interactions, where gestures and context assist comprehension, the phone strips away visual cues and accelerates speech. Yet phone Japanese follows set frameworks that, once mastered, provide confidence. Answering a call may begin with your name followed by でございます in formal settings or a simple もしもし among friends. For deliveries, staff often confirm addresses or times, asking ご在宅でしょうか? or お届けは何時ごろご希望ですか? Reservations at restaurants or clinics usually follow a predictable script: stating your name, number of people, date and time, and any special requests. 予約をお願いしたいのですが signals politely that you wish to make a booking.

Customer service calls require an extra layer of formality. Phrases like 少々お待ちください signal a brief hold, while 確認いたします assures you that the staff are checking details. For learners, these calls may seem like linguistic minefields, but the formulaic structure actually provides security. By memorizing key phrases and practicing them aloud, you prepare for ninety percent of the situations you will face. Even if comprehension falters, recognizing anchor phrases gives you enough to navigate.

What unites these daily interactions—conbini, restaurants, phones—is their reliance on set expressions that differ from textbook examples but recur with reliable consistency. They are the true currency of everyday Japanese, phrases that smooth transactions and signal cultural belonging. Mastering them requires more than passive recognition. It requires rehearsal, active use, and the humility to learn from mistakes. Each interaction becomes both a challenge and an opportunity.

The learner who walks into a convenience store for the first time may freeze at the cashier's rapid questions. By the tenth visit, they respond smoothly, even anticipating the next phrase. The diner who once stumbled over ordering learns to say 水をお願いします without hesitation, earning a nod of understanding. The nervous caller who once dreaded the phone eventually makes a reservation with confidence, even handling clarifications politely. These transformations are the milestones of true fluency—not the ability to translate complex essays, but the ability to function seamlessly in ordinary life.

Daily life interactions matter because they represent the bridge between formal study and lived reality. They are the moments where Japanese stops being a subject and becomes a tool. The sooner learners embrace these encounters, the sooner they shed the artificial layer of classroom speech and step into authentic communication. Beyond "How are you?" lies the real Japan, with its conbini counters, restaurant tables, and telephone lines, waiting for you to speak with clarity and confidence.

## 6.2 Social Dynamics: Reading the Air (空気を読む)

One of the defining features of Japanese communication is its subtlety. While Western cultures often value directness as a sign of honesty, Japanese society tends to prioritize harmony, preferring expressions that maintain relationships and avoid confrontation. The phrase *空気を読む*, literally "to read the air," captures this ethos. It refers to the unspoken skill of sensing context, interpreting what is left unsaid, and responding in ways that preserve balance. For learners, understanding this principle is as important as learning vocabulary or grammar. Without it, words may be accurate but socially tone-deaf.

A prime example is how refusals are expressed. In English, saying "no" is straightforward, even expected. In Japanese, the word いいえ exists, but it is rarely used in situations where it would sound blunt or create discomfort. Instead, refusals are often delivered indirectly, using softening strategies. A common phrase is ちょっと…, trailing off without finishing the sentence. The implication is clear to a Japanese listener: "I cannot" or "it is difficult," but the refusal is framed gently, leaving space for the other person to save face. Another strategy is 考えておきます, literally "I'll think about it." While it sounds like a promise to consider, in practice it often means a polite "no." These expressions embody the cultural preference for ambiguity, where the message is conveyed without sharp edges. For learners, adopting such techniques prevents misunderstandings and signals sensitivity to the subtleties of social interaction.

Gift-giving is another area where *reading the air* plays a crucial role. In Japan, gifts are not just tokens of affection but structured acts governed by vocabulary and ritual. When traveling, it is customary to bring back おみやげ, souvenirs for colleagues, friends, or family. Upon receiving a gift, etiquette dictates offering お返し, a reciprocal gift, often of lesser or equal value, to acknowledge the gesture. When presenting a gift, people often downplay its value, saying つまらないものですが, "it's nothing special, but please accept it." Far from being literal, this phrase reflects humility, a way of lowering oneself to elevate the receiver. For learners, mastering this language of gifts reveals not only politeness but also the cultural rhythm of reciprocity that underpins social bonds.

Apologies provide yet another window into the social fabric. In English, "sorry" covers a wide range of contexts, from bumping into someone to committing a serious mistake. Japanese, however, employs a spectrum of apologies, each calibrated to situation and relationship. すみません is versatile, used not only to apologize but also to gain attention or express gratitude. ごめんなさい leans toward personal apologies, often among friends or equals. At the most formal level, 申し訳ございません conveys deep remorse, appropriate in business or when a serious mistake has occurred. Choosing the right form is not simply about semantics—it reflects social awareness. An overly formal apology among friends may sound stiff, while a casual one in business may appear disrespectful. Understanding this spectrum allows learners to navigate interactions with nuance, acknowledging mistakes in ways that strengthen rather than weaken trust.

Taken together, indirect refusals, gift-giving customs, and layered apologies illustrate what 空気を読む truly means. It is the ability to respond not only with correct words but with words that fit the social atmosphere. It requires sensitivity to context, awareness of hierarchy, and a willingness to prioritize harmony over blunt expression. For learners, practicing this skill transforms communication from mechanical to authentic. It is the difference between speaking Japanese and living Japanese.

# 6.3 Professional Japanese: Workplace Communication

If social dynamics demand sensitivity, professional contexts demand precision. The Japanese workplace operates within a framework of etiquette that governs how people write, speak, and present themselves. For learners aiming to use Japanese professionally, mastering this framework is essential. It is not enough to know how to form sentences; you must know how to frame them in ways that show respect, clarity, and competence.

Business emails, for example, follow a set structure that may seem formulaic but carries great weight. A typical opening is お世話になっております, a phrase that literally means "I am indebted to your care." It functions as a ritual acknowledgment of the relationship, signaling humility and gratitude. The body of the email is often concise, avoiding unnecessary elaboration, yet always framed politely. Closings commonly use よろしくお願いいたします, a phrase that defies direct translation but conveys a request for favorable consideration. For learners, memorizing these templates provides a safety net, ensuring that even when vocabulary is limited, the tone remains professional.

Meetings present a different challenge. Speaking up requires not only language but also timing. To express an opinion, phrases like 私の考えでは ("in my opinion") or 私としては ("from my perspective") provide polite entry points. Building on others' contributions requires acknowledgment before offering your own, as in なるほど、それに加えて ("I see, and in addition to that"). These expressions prevent speech from sounding confrontational, reinforcing the collaborative spirit of Japanese discussions. Silence also plays a role. Pausing before speaking or after listening signals reflection, not hesitation, and demonstrates respect for the collective flow of conversation.

Self-introductions, or 自己紹介, are another cornerstone of workplace communication. Beyond stating your name, position, and affiliation, the challenge lies in adjusting length and content to context. A thirty-second version may suffice in casual networking, a one-minute version in formal meetings, and a three-minute version when addressing a larger group. The balance lies in being professional yet personable. Mentioning your department and role is expected, but adding a brief detail about your motivation or background creates connection. Phrases like どうぞよろしくお願いいたします close the introduction, signaling willingness to cooperate and respect for the group.

Professional Japanese also reflects the layered politeness system of the language, particularly 敬語 (honorific speech). While full mastery requires years, even partial awareness earns respect. Knowing when to elevate the listener's actions with 尊敬語—such as using いらっしゃる instead of 行く—or when to humble your own actions with 謙譲語—using 伺う instead of 行く when visiting—shows sensitivity to hierarchy. In workplaces where relationships are carefully structured, these distinctions carry weight. They are not just linguistic flourishes but signals of professionalism and awareness.

For learners, the leap from textbooks to professional Japanese may feel immense. Yet much like convenience store conversations or restaurant interactions, workplace communication thrives on predictable patterns. Emails follow templates. Meetings rely on recurring phrases. Introductions follow structured outlines. By studying these frameworks and rehearsing them, learners gain confidence. The goal is not to improvise eloquently from day one but to enter professional spaces equipped with tools that work reliably.

Ultimately, professional Japanese is about trust. When you write an email with proper openings and closings, you show respect for the relationship. When you contribute in a meeting with acknowledgment and clarity, you show respect for the collective process. When you introduce yourself with humility and confidence, you show respect for the group you are joining. These gestures matter as much as the content itself. They reveal that you are not merely speaking Japanese—you are participating in Japanese professional culture.

# Chapter 7: Cultural Intelligence – The Unwritten Rules of Japanese Communication

*"In Japan, 93% of communication is non-verbal, compared to 55% in Western cultures – mastering context is as crucial as vocabulary."*

## 7.1 High-Context Communication Patterns

Language is not just grammar and vocabulary; it is the cultural air people breathe. Nowhere is this truer than in Japan, where the mechanics of speech are only part of the message. The rest emerges from silence, tone, facial expression, and an intricate dance of context. To master Japanese, one must master this invisible layer of meaning. Without it, words risk being hollow shells, technically correct yet socially off-key. This is the essence of high-context communication, where the true meaning often lies not in what is spoken but in what is left unsaid.

Central to this high-context world is the distinction between 本音 (honne) and 建前 (tatemae). *Honne* represents one's genuine feelings or desires, while *tatemae* represents the socially acceptable facade presented in public. These two forces coexist constantly, shaping conversations in ways that puzzle many learners. When a Japanese colleague says, 検討しておきます —"I will think about it"—a literal-minded learner may expect an actual decision to follow. But often, the phrase serves as *tatemae*, a polite refusal cloaked in consideration. The *honne* is "no," but voicing it directly would disrupt harmony. Recognizing this duality is not about assuming dishonesty but about understanding the cultural emphasis on smooth relationships.

This interplay extends to daily interactions. An invitation to dinner may receive a response like また今度—"next time"—which often implies that the person does not plan to accept. Similarly, hesitation markers such as ちょっと or elongated pauses can communicate refusal without ever using the blunt word "no." Learners who take these expressions at face value risk waiting indefinitely for follow-ups that will never come. By contrast, those who attune themselves to *honne* and *tatemae* begin to hear the music beneath the words, perceiving intention where none is spoken outright.

What is unsaid often matters more than what is spoken. This is where the concepts of 遠慮 (enryo, restraint) and 察する (sassuru, to guess or sense) come into play. In Japanese culture, restraint is a virtue, and explicit self-assertion can be seen as disruptive. Instead of voicing needs directly, people often expect others to *sassuru*, to intuit from context. A guest at a dinner who says, もう結構です, literally "I'm fine," may still want more food but refrains out of politeness. The host, reading the air, may offer again, gauging body language and tone. In this way, interaction becomes a negotiation of subtle cues rather than explicit statements.

For learners accustomed to low-context cultures, where clarity and directness are praised, this can be frustrating. Yet learning to operate in this high-context environment is transformative. It forces you to listen not only with your ears but with your eyes and intuition. You notice pauses, shifts in tone, sidelong glances, and even the strategic use of silence. In Japanese, silence is not an absence of communication but a form of it. A pause can convey agreement, resistance, or contemplation. The challenge lies in discerning which it is, and the answer often depends on the situation more than the words themselves.

Developing situational awareness is therefore essential. In Japan, the same words can carry entirely different meanings depending on who speaks them, where, and to whom. Saying お疲れ様です to a colleague at the end of the day signals camaraderie, but saying it to a superior too early in the day might seem presumptuous, as though you are implying they are finished with work. A casual phrase among friends can be inappropriate in a formal meeting, while a stiff expression in a casual setting may come across as cold. Registers of speech are not chosen in isolation but calibrated to context: workplace hierarchies, age differences, and even whether one is speaking face-to-face or on the phone all shape the proper register.

Consider the role of non-verbal cues. In a business meeting, a simple nod may not indicate agreement but acknowledgment that the message has been received. A smile may not always mean amusement but could mask discomfort or polite restraint. Even posture matters; leaning forward slightly shows engagement, while excessive gesturing may feel disruptive. Learning to read these cues is not a matter of mimicking Japanese people mechanically but of sensitizing yourself to the patterns that underlie their interactions.

The learner who masters this sensitivity finds that conversations once confusing begin to make sense. What sounded like evasive vagueness reveals itself as an elegant system for maintaining harmony. Phrases that seemed empty—また今度, 考えておきます, 結構です—become rich with layers of meaning once filtered through context. You no longer feel lost when someone avoids a direct answer, because you understand that the answer was already given, just not in words.

This does not mean abandoning your own cultural instincts but expanding them. As a bilingual speaker moves between languages, you as a learner move between communication styles. In English, clarity might mean saying exactly what you mean. In Japanese, clarity often means ensuring that your message preserves the relationship, even if that requires indirection. Mastery of Japanese communication lies not in imposing one system on the other but in flexibly navigating both.

High-context communication also shapes group dynamics. In meetings, decisions may not be voiced explicitly but emerge from a gradual convergence of unspoken agreement. Participants may avoid confrontation, preferring to let silence signal consensus. For learners, the temptation is to fill silence with words or to press for direct answers. But patience often reveals that the silence was the answer. By observing carefully, you begin to see how collective decision-making unfolds in subtle ways, without the explicit markers you might expect.

The challenge of learning these unwritten rules can be daunting, but it also offers one of the deepest rewards of studying Japanese. Vocabulary and grammar open doors to communication, but cultural intelligence opens doors to trust and belonging. When you demonstrate sensitivity to *honne* and *tatemae*, when you respond with restraint rather than insistence, when you respect silence as communication, you show that you understand not just the language but the culture that gives it life.

In the end, high-context communication is less about deciphering secret codes and more about developing empathy. It requires slowing down, observing carefully, and recognizing that meaning lives not only in words but in the spaces around them. For learners, cultivating this awareness transforms interactions from baffling exchanges into meaningful dialogues. It is the skill that allows you not just to speak Japanese but to participate in Japanese society, where what is not said often speaks the loudest.

# 7.2 Social Hierarchy Navigation

Japanese society is often described as vertical, and while such simplifications risk exaggeration, it is undeniable that hierarchy permeates communication at every level. To speak Japanese fluently is not merely to choose the right verbs or particles but to adjust constantly to one's social position relative to others. This is not a rigid system of dominance but a living network of respect, reciprocity, and awareness.

One of the most prominent expressions of this hierarchy is the *senpai–kohai* relationship. In schools, companies, clubs, and even casual social groups, those with greater age or experience hold the role of *senpai*, while juniors or newcomers take the role of *kohai*. This dynamic influences not only behavior but also language. A *kohai* is expected to use polite speech when addressing a *senpai*, while the *senpai* may respond in a more relaxed register. The exchange of greetings, the choice of verbs, even the timing of when one speaks, all shift depending on these roles. To misunderstand this dynamic is not merely a linguistic slip; it risks being seen as disrespectful or ignorant of social norms. Yet when learners observe and adapt, they gain a valuable tool for integration.

Closely related is the distinction between *uchi* (inside) and *soto* (outside), categories that extend beyond family into companies, schools, and communities. The *uchi* group represents those considered insiders, while *soto* refers to outsiders. Language adjusts accordingly. When introducing your company to an external client, you might speak humbly about your own organization, even lowering its status through humble forms of verbs, while elevating the client's company with honorific speech. Thus, the same action—say, a superior "coming" to a meeting—might be expressed differently depending on perspective: いらっしゃる when describing the client's action, 参る when referring to one's own colleague. This system forces speakers to constantly orient themselves within shifting circles of relationship, a process that may seem exhausting to outsiders but which Japanese speakers navigate instinctively.

The choreography of business card exchange illustrates hierarchy in motion. When two professionals meet for the first time, they bow slightly, present their cards with both hands, and accompany the gesture with polite phrases such as よろしくお願いいたします or はじめまして. The card is received with both hands, studied briefly, and often placed respectfully on the table during the meeting rather than tucked immediately away. The position of the cards on the table itself can mirror hierarchy, with the senior person's card placed in the most prominent location. These small acts are not superficial ritual but embodied respect, affirming awareness of the relationship being established. For a learner entering Japanese business culture, mastering this choreography communicates seriousness and understanding before a single substantive word is spoken.

Hierarchy is not static but situational. In one context, you may be the junior, deferring to a superior. In another, you may hold seniority, and the language adjusts accordingly. The art lies in recognizing cues: age, position, group membership, and context. Japanese society rarely announces these explicitly, but the attentive learner begins to discern them. Titles, introductions, and even seating arrangements all provide signals. By observing carefully, you learn not just which words to choose but which stance to adopt. This awareness transforms interactions from mechanical exchanges into socially attuned communication.

## 7.3 Seasonal and Ceremonial Language

If hierarchy shapes vertical relationships in Japanese communication, seasonality and ceremony shape its rhythm. Language in Japan is deeply tied to the cycles of nature and the formalities of life's milestones. To speak Japanese well is to participate in this shared calendar, aligning greetings, phrases, and expressions with the changing seasons and with the ceremonial occasions that mark existence.

Season-specific greetings are one of the most distinctive features. At New Year, people exchange 明けましておめでとうございます, wishing each other congratulations for the arrival of a new year. In the heat of summer, letters and emails may begin with 暑中お見舞い申し上げます, a seasonal salutation acknowledging the oppressive weather while expressing concern for the recipient's health. In autumn, conversations often include comments on the beauty of the leaves, while winter greetings may mention the cold and encourage the listener to take care. These phrases may seem formulaic, but they serve as cultural glue, reaffirming shared experience and mutual care through the passing of time. For learners, adopting such greetings is not about parroting fixed expressions but about stepping into the rhythm of life as Japanese people experience it.

Ceremonial occasions add another layer of linguistic richness. Weddings, for example, are accompanied by phrases that emphasize joy and blessing, such as ご結婚おめでとうございます. Funerals, by contrast, demand subdued expressions of condolence, such as ご愁傷様でございます. Coming-of-age ceremonies prompt congratulations that acknowledge both individual achievement and entry into adult responsibility. Workplace events, from promotions to retirements, likewise carry their own vocabulary, with phrases that balance congratulations with humility, ensuring the focus is placed not on self but on collective harmony. Each of these occasions requires not just the right words but the right tone, a balance of warmth, respect, and sensitivity.

Food culture provides perhaps the most daily but also most profound examples of ceremonial language. Before eating, people say いただきます, literally "I humbly receive." After finishing, they say ごちそうさまでした, thanking not only the cook but the life and labor that provided the meal. These expressions go beyond politeness; they reflect a worldview in which gratitude is woven into daily sustenance. Dining etiquette includes additional phrases: offering a toast with 乾杯, apologizing for eating before others with お先にいただきます, or complimenting the meal with 美味しいです. Each phrase situates the speaker within a community of respect, turning eating from a private act into a shared ritual.

For learners, mastering seasonal and ceremonial language is not just a matter of expanding vocabulary but of entering the cultural consciousness. It signals awareness that words are not neutral carriers of meaning but part of a web of traditions, expectations, and shared values. A simple phrase timed correctly can transform an interaction, showing that you are not merely a foreigner who knows grammar but a participant who understands the deeper layers of communication.

Together, social hierarchy and ceremonial language reveal the extent to which Japanese communication transcends words alone. They show how language encodes respect, harmony, seasonality, and ritual. To navigate this world requires more than memorization. It requires sensitivity, observation, and practice. But for those who embrace these dimensions, Japanese opens not just as a language but as a way of seeing and living, where meaning flows as much from silence, timing, and ritual as from vocabulary and grammar.

# Chapter 8: Digital Japanese – Navigating Technology and Online Spaces

*"Japanese internet users have created over 10,000 unique emoticons (kaomoji) and abbreviations, forming a digital dialect that's essential for online communication."*

## 8.1 Typing and Digital Input Methods

For centuries, Japanese was written with brush, pen, or printing blocks, its flowing strokes demanding patience and precision. Yet in the digital age, the language has adapted to keyboards, touchscreens, and predictive algorithms. For learners, this digital revolution is both a blessing and a challenge. On one hand, you no longer need to memorize thousands of kanji stroke orders just to write a message. On the other, typing Japanese requires mastering a system that bridges two writing traditions: the Roman alphabet and the kana–kanji script. Understanding this system is not optional—it is central to functioning in modern Japan, where most communication, from texting to professional emails, happens through digital devices.

At the core of Japanese digital writing lies the Input Method Editor, or IME. This software acts as a translator between the Latin alphabet, which most keyboards use, and the Japanese syllabaries. When you type *arigatou* on a keyboard, the IME converts it into hiragana: ありがとう. With a keystroke, you can then transform it into kanji or mixed writing, if appropriate. This process is known as romaji-to-hiragana conversion, and while it may sound straightforward, true mastery requires practice and optimization.

Beginners often type slowly, searching for each syllable, waiting for the IME to offer suggestions. But experienced users harness shortcuts that triple their typing speed. For example, knowing that typing "nn" produces ん prevents the system from creating unwanted combinations. Shortcuts like "ltu" or "xtu" produce the small っ used for double consonants, essential for accurate spelling. Mastery involves not just memorizing these codes but training your fingers to glide through them until hiragana streams onto the screen as smoothly as English words. Adjusting IME settings also plays a crucial role. By fine-tuning prediction behavior, customizing dictionaries with frequently used names or terms, and learning hotkeys to toggle between input modes, you can transform the IME from a stumbling block into a powerful ally.

Beyond basic conversion lies the world of predictive text, where the IME suggests kanji and phrases based on frequency patterns. Japanese, with its thousands of homophones, relies heavily on context to determine the correct kanji. Type "hashi," and the system may offer 橋 (bridge), 箸 (chopsticks), or 端 (edge). The predictive engine, drawing on usage statistics, often places the most common choice first. Over time, it adapts to your personal patterns, learning which words you select most often. This predictive feature, far from being a mere convenience, is essential for fluent digital writing. Without it, you would spend endless time scrolling through lists of kanji, hunting for the right one. With it, writing becomes fast, natural, and almost conversational.

Learning to exploit predictive text also means paying attention to phrases rather than isolated words. IMEs recognize collocations and common expressions, offering full suggestions after only a few keystrokes. Typing "omedeto" might instantly bring up おめでとうございます, saving time and ensuring accuracy. In this way, the system itself becomes a teacher, reinforcing the most natural forms of expression. The learner who engages actively with these suggestions accelerates not only typing speed but also linguistic intuition, internalizing patterns through daily digital practice.

The shift from computers to smartphones adds another layer of complexity. While keyboards dominate on desktops and laptops, most Japanese today type on mobile devices, where space is limited and efficiency paramount. Here, the preferred method is *flick input* (フリック入力). Instead of pressing keys for each syllable, users tap or swipe in specific directions on a grid where each vowel surrounds a consonant. To type か, you press once; to type き, you swipe upward; for く, swipe right; for け, swipe down; and for こ, swipe left. This method dramatically reduces keystrokes once mastered, making it faster than tapping through every kana individually.

At first, flick input can feel alien to learners accustomed to QWERTY layouts. Yet it mirrors the rhythmic efficiency prized in Japanese communication. Mastery comes from repetition—practicing common words, building muscle memory until swipes become instinctive. The payoff is enormous: native speakers who use flick input can type at remarkable speed, sometimes rivaling or surpassing their desktop efficiency. Learners who embrace this system not only communicate faster but also align themselves with the habits of everyday Japanese users.

Mobile devices also offer voice-to-text functions, an increasingly common tool in a society that values efficiency. Japanese voice input is remarkably accurate, capable of distinguishing homophones through context and punctuation through simple verbal cues. Saying "ten" inserts a period, while "kakko" adds parentheses. For learners, voice input can serve as both a practical tool and a pronunciation check. If the system fails to recognize your words, it often means your accent or pitch is off. By practicing until the voice-to-text transcribes accurately, you refine your spoken Japanese while preparing messages at the same time. Yet, as with any tool, appropriateness matters. Voice input is convenient in private or casual settings but less suitable in public spaces or professional contexts, where typing remains the norm.

Digital input methods are not just technical tricks; they shape the way Japanese is written today. In earlier generations, limited by handwriting, people often relied on simpler kanji or kana. Now, with predictive text, complex kanji are only a keystroke away, preserving richness without slowing communication. This shift also means that literacy today involves not just knowing how to write characters by hand but how to navigate digital systems effectively. A learner who clings only to handwriting risks isolation from modern Japanese life, where even quick notes, shopping lists, and diary entries are often typed on phones.

The digital transformation also influences social expression. The ease of typing kana encourages abbreviations and slang, especially among younger users. Predictive text generates not only standard forms but also internet neologisms, expanding your exposure to the living language. Meanwhile, kaomoji—emoticons built from Japanese characters—flow directly from IME inputs, offering a visual dimension to text. A simple (´・ω・`) conveys sadness, while (´ヴ`) radiates joy. These digital flourishes, born of Japanese input systems, now define much of the nation's online communication.

For learners, embracing digital input is not merely about convenience. It is about legitimacy. Typing fluently, choosing the right kanji swiftly, and responding naturally in chats or emails signals to native speakers that you belong in the digital space of modern Japan. Without this ability, you risk being perceived as permanently "in learner mode," unable to function in the actual arenas where language now lives.

The journey toward mastering digital input is not linear. At first, you will type slowly, stumble over romaji conversions, and misselect kanji. But each mistake is part of the process. Over time, your IME adapts to you, your hands adapt to flick input, and your brain adapts to predictive suggestions. What once felt mechanical becomes intuitive, as natural as writing in English. This mastery is not an afterthought to language learning—it is the foundation of participation in twenty-first-century Japanese life.

## 8.2 Online Communication Culture

Japanese communication has always prized nuance, brevity, and indirectness, and these qualities have adapted seamlessly into the digital age. On the internet, where character limits, speed, and casualness shape conversation, Japanese users have developed a culture that feels at once familiar and distinctly their own. To participate meaningfully in this space, learners must understand not just the language but the conventions of each platform, the shortcuts of slang, and the unspoken grammar of emoji and kaomoji.

Take *LINE*, Japan's dominant messaging app. Unlike Western counterparts like WhatsApp or Messenger, LINE integrates stickers, character-based themes, and group chats into everyday communication. A single sticker of a cartoon bear bowing may replace an entire sentence of apology, while an animated image of a character cheering can substitute for encouragement. The platform fosters an atmosphere where visual language complements text, reinforcing tone without requiring lengthy explanations. Messages tend to be short, casual, and rapid-fire, with participants often sending multiple lines instead of one long block. For learners, mastering LINE etiquette—when to use stickers, how often to respond, how casual the tone can be—becomes a gateway to authentic social interaction.

Twitter in Japan is another unique space. Despite the platform's global presence, Japanese users employ it differently. Character limits encourage concise posts, often filled with abbreviations or clipped phrases. Hashtags serve not only to mark topics but also to participate in ongoing collective conversations, such as seasonal events, television shows, or breaking news. Unlike in English Twitter, where sarcasm and irony dominate, Japanese Twitter often blends sincerity with coded humor, creating layers of meaning accessible only to those familiar with cultural references and shorthand. Learners who engage with Twitter discover a constant stream of living Japanese, from political commentary to casual observations, shaped by the rhythm of brevity.

Other social media platforms carry their own conventions. Instagram captions often lean poetic or playful, with hashtags linking posts into communities of interest, from travel and food to fashion and hobbies. TikTok videos feature captions that condense jokes or trends into a handful of characters. YouTube comment sections showcase casual speech, peppered with slang, abbreviations, and emoji, giving learners insight into how Japanese is used informally by younger generations. Each platform becomes not only a tool for connection but a classroom for observing how digital Japanese evolves in real time.

Central to this online communication culture is the extensive use of slang and abbreviations. Japanese has always valued efficiency, and digital spaces amplify this instinct. Common phrases shrink into shorthand: 了解 (understood) contracts to りょ, while お疲れ様 (thank you for your effort) becomes おつ. These clipped forms, though informal, are ubiquitous among friends and peers online. Acronyms also proliferate. JK, short for 女子高生, literally "high school girl," appears in casual conversations, advertisements, and memes. Other abbreviations mark pop culture references, relationship statuses, or inside jokes. For the uninitiated, these strings of letters and symbols may look impenetrable, but with exposure, they reveal themselves as part of a living dialect, one that constantly shifts as new slang emerges.

Emoji and kaomoji form the emotional grammar of Japanese digital speech. Unlike Western emoji, which often depict objects or simplified faces, Japanese users pioneered kaomoji, elaborate text-based emoticons that capture moods with surprising nuance. A simple (´・ω・`) conveys sadness or disappointment, while \(^o^)/ bursts with joy. More dramatic expressions like (╯°□°)╯ represent frustration or exaggerated emotion. These symbols are not random decorations but integral components of communication, softening blunt statements, adding playfulness, or clarifying tone. Without them, text risks sounding cold or overly serious. Learners who adopt them begin to grasp not only how Japanese people express themselves online but how they manage relationships through digital tone.

In this sense, the internet functions as both mirror and amplifier of Japanese cultural traits. Indirectness finds expression in abbreviations that leave meaning half-spoken. Politeness appears in the ubiquity of おつ after shared online efforts, whether gaming sessions or group projects. Community emerges through hashtags that link individuals into collective conversations. Digital Japanese is not a departure from tradition but its evolution, reshaped by technology yet still carrying the values of brevity, harmony, and shared understanding. For learners, immersing in this culture means more than decoding slang. It means learning to inhabit a digital dialect that reveals the living pulse of the language.

## 8.3 Digital Resources and Learning Tools

If online communication shows how Japanese is lived, digital resources show how it can be learned. Never before have learners had access to such a wide ecosystem of tools, each offering unique pathways into vocabulary, grammar, and conversation. The challenge is no longer scarcity but choice—navigating apps, websites, and media to craft a personal learning strategy that balances efficiency with depth.

Language exchange apps like HelloTalk, Tandem, and italki have transformed practice opportunities. HelloTalk connects learners with native speakers for text, audio, and voice messages, often with built-in correction tools that allow partners to edit each other's sentences. Tandem offers similar features, focusing on conversation partners matched by interest or proficiency. italki goes further by providing access to professional tutors for structured lessons, blending casual practice with formal instruction. Each platform carries its own culture: HelloTalk encourages playful exchanges, Tandem emphasizes community, while italki mirrors the classroom in digital form. Learners can move between them depending on their goals, shifting from free conversation to guided learning with ease.

Dictionaries, once thick tomes, now thrive online with unparalleled functionality. Jisho.org stands out as a comprehensive resource, combining radical lookup, stroke order diagrams, example sentences, JLPT level indicators, and audio. The radical search is particularly valuable for kanji learners: even when you cannot identify the whole character, you can break it into components and find it efficiently. Example sentences ground vocabulary in real use, preventing the trap of memorizing words without context. By bookmarking or exporting entries, learners can build personalized lexicons, turning Jisho into both a reference and a study companion.

YouTube and podcasts offer another dimension: immersion through comprehensible input. Channels like *Japanese Ammo with Misa* present grammar and vocabulary in engaging, accessible ways, blending explanation with examples drawn from everyday life. Other creators specialize in storytelling, cultural commentary, or news, catering to different proficiency levels. Podcasts range from beginner-friendly slow Japanese to advanced discussions of current events. The key lies in curation: selecting sources slightly above your current level, so that each listening session stretches comprehension without overwhelming. Over time, these resources replicate the effect of living in Japan, surrounding you with language until comprehension becomes instinctive.

Digital resources also allow learners to personalize their journey. Some may thrive on structured lessons with tutors, others on self-directed reading of online articles, still others on listening to podcasts during commutes. Unlike the rigidity of traditional classrooms, the digital ecosystem adapts to the learner's lifestyle, making it possible to integrate Japanese study into daily routines. Five minutes on an app during a break, a podcast during a jog, a YouTube lesson before bed—each moment adds to a mosaic of exposure that accumulates into fluency.

What unites these tools is their accessibility. No matter where you live, you can connect with native speakers, access dictionaries once available only in Japan, and immerse yourself in content produced for real audiences. This democratization of learning removes the old barriers of geography and cost. Yet it also demands responsibility: with so many choices, discipline and consistency matter more than ever. The learner who dabbles without focus risks being overwhelmed, while the one who crafts a plan—balancing speaking, listening, reading, and writing—harnesses the full power of the digital age.

For those serious about Japanese mastery, digital tools are not a supplement but the foundation of progress. They offer exposure, correction, explanation, and practice, all at a scale unimaginable a generation ago. To ignore them is to handicap yourself; to embrace them is to accelerate your journey. With the right combination of apps, dictionaries, and media, you can create a personalized immersion environment that rivals living in Japan itself.

# Chapter 9: The JLPT Roadmap – Structured Milestones to Fluency

*"Over 1 million people worldwide take the JLPT annually, with N3 level holders qualifying for most Japanese university programs and N2 opening professional opportunities."*

## 9.1 Strategic JLPT Preparation Timeline

The Japanese Language Proficiency Test, known universally as the JLPT, has become more than an examination. It is a global benchmark, a structured ladder that offers both learners and institutions a clear sense of progress. For students, it provides milestones and motivation. For universities and employers, it serves as a reliable measure of competence. Unlike casual self-assessment, the JLPT offers an external standard recognized in Japan and abroad. Preparing for it requires not only dedication but also strategy, because the test is not simply about whether you can "use Japanese" in everyday life. It measures specific skills under time pressure, with formats that differ from natural conversation or writing. Understanding this distinction is critical for building a preparation plan that is both realistic and effective.

The roadmap begins with N5, the introductory level. On average, learners need around 150 hours of focused study to reach this stage. At N5, you are expected to recognize about 100 kanji and 800 words, alongside basic grammar and everyday expressions. It is the level of survival Japanese—introducing yourself, understanding simple written directions, reading menus with support. For some, N5 represents a confidence-building milestone rather than a professional qualification. The timeline for reaching it can be as short as six months for part-time learners or as little as three months for intensive study.

Progressing to N4 typically requires doubling that effort, around 300 hours of structured practice. At this stage, learners expand to about 300 kanji and 1,500 vocabulary items. N4 covers the territory of extended daily conversation: talking about family, work routines, hobbies, and basic written communication. While N4 is not widely recognized by universities or companies, it provides the scaffolding for intermediate fluency. Students who reach this level often find that they can travel in Japan with comfort, understand simple signage, and carry out transactions without depending on English.

The transition to N3 marks the shift from beginner to intermediate proficiency, demanding about 450 hours in total. Here, vocabulary grows to roughly 3,000 words and kanji recognition surpasses 600. N3 opens doors academically, as many universities accept it for enrollment, recognizing that learners at this stage can follow lectures with support. It also represents the threshold where Japanese begins to feel like a living skill rather than a study subject. You can read short articles, follow dramas with partial understanding, and participate in conversations that extend beyond immediate needs. Achieving N3 often takes one to two years of consistent study, depending on intensity.

N2, requiring about 600 hours, is widely considered the professional gateway. It signifies command of 6,000 words and around 1,000 kanji, enabling comprehension of newspapers, formal documents, and business correspondence. Many companies in Japan set N2 as the minimum requirement for employment in positions that require Japanese. At this level, the learner is not merely surviving but functioning independently, capable of handling complex conversations, grasping nuance, and reading most non-specialist materials. The leap from N3 to

N2 is steep, demanding not only vocabulary expansion but a sharper grasp of grammar, nuance, and speed reading under exam conditions.

Finally, N1 stands at the summit, requiring 900 hours or more. Holders of N1 can navigate academic papers, literature, and professional environments without significant barriers. N1 is less about practical necessity—since N2 often suffices for work or study—and more about demonstrating mastery. It is a credential that signals to universities, employers, and peers that you have achieved near-native competence in reading, listening, and analyzing Japanese. Reaching N1 can take several years even for motivated learners, as the complexity of vocabulary and the density of reading passages test not just language but stamina and discipline.

Yet timelines and vocabulary counts alone do not ensure success. The JLPT differs from real-world Japanese in crucial ways. The test does not measure speaking or writing directly. Instead, it emphasizes reading comprehension, listening comprehension, grammar, and vocabulary recognition. This means that a learner who speaks fluently may still struggle on the exam if they cannot parse long reading passages or quickly identify the correct kanji from multiple options. Conversely, someone who masters the exam format may score well while still finding casual conversation challenging. Preparation, therefore, must be adapted to the test's particular style.

Understanding JLPT question design is essential. Reading passages often contain distractor options that test not only comprehension but attention to nuance. Listening sections move quickly, with limited repetition, forcing learners to retain key details under time pressure. Grammar questions frequently test subtle distinctions between similar expressions, requiring precision beyond what daily conversation demands. Adapting to these formats means training specifically for the exam rather than assuming that general language study will suffice. Practice with past papers, official mock exams, and JLPT-specific textbooks is indispensable for building familiarity and speed.

Mock test analysis forms the backbone of serious preparation. Taking a practice exam under timed conditions reveals more than vocabulary gaps; it exposes patterns of weakness. Some learners discover they read too slowly, failing to finish the reading section despite understanding the passages. Others realize their listening comprehension falters not because of vocabulary but because they miss the structure of questions. By dissecting errors systematically, you can create targeted improvement plans. If you consistently misinterpret grammar items, you know to revisit specific points. If kanji recognition slows you down, you focus on high-frequency characters. The test becomes less a mystery and more a predictable challenge.

Creating a preparation timeline also involves pacing. For beginners, setting sights on N5 within the first year provides motivation and a tangible goal. For those aiming higher, it is important to recognize that each level requires exponentially more effort than the last. Attempting to leap from N5 to N2 in a year is unrealistic and risks burnout. Instead, aligning study schedules with the expected hours for each stage provides structure without discouragement. Learners who balance steady progress with realistic milestones sustain momentum far more effectively than those who rush only to stumble.

At the same time, flexibility is crucial. Timelines are averages, not destiny. Some learners may reach N3 within a year through immersion, while others may take three years due to work or family commitments. The important measure is consistency. Even an hour a day accumulates into hundreds of hours annually, enough to move from beginner to intermediate. The test rewards persistence as much as aptitude.

Ultimately, the JLPT roadmap is less about certification alone and more about structuring the journey toward fluency. It provides external validation but also internal motivation. By breaking the vast challenge of Japanese into stages—N5 survival, N4 foundation, N3 independence, N2 professionalism, N1 mastery—you create a ladder to climb rather than a cliff to scale. Each step builds confidence, each certificate proves progress, and each exam cycle turns preparation into achievement.

For learners, the key is to approach the JLPT strategically: know the timeline, understand the exam's unique demands, analyze practice results, and adjust accordingly. In doing so, you not only prepare for a test but also refine the skills that support real-world fluency. Passing the JLPT becomes not just a credential but a reflection of a disciplined, structured approach to mastering Japanese.

## 9.2 Beyond Test Prep: Practical Proficiency

The JLPT provides structure and credibility, but anyone who has taken the exam and then tried to live or work in Japan quickly realizes that the certificate alone does not guarantee fluency. The test has a narrow focus: it measures reading comprehension, listening skills, vocabulary recognition, and grammar. It does not evaluate speaking or writing, nor does it measure how well you can navigate the fluid unpredictability of real interactions. This creates what many call the "JLPT gap"—the difference between test performance and practical proficiency. Bridging that gap requires deliberate effort, supplementing preparation with experiences and practices that go beyond the exam's scope.

One of the most effective ways to close this gap is incorporating authentic materials into your study routine. JLPT textbooks, while essential for mastering the exam format, often present artificially simplified passages. Real-world Japanese, however, appears in forms like news articles, novels, television shows, podcasts, and social media. These sources are messy, filled with slang, abbreviations, cultural references, and sentence structures that the exam will not test but that daily life demands you understand. Reading an NHK news article, for instance, not only challenges your vocabulary but forces you to parse formal grammar structures. Watching a drama exposes you to rapid-fire speech patterns, interruptions, and unfinished sentences—features common in conversation but absent from textbooks. By balancing exam drills with exposure to these materials, you train yourself to operate in both the controlled world of the test and the unpredictable world of reality.

The second challenge is the output deficit. Because the JLPT does not measure speaking or writing, many learners neglect them in favor of reading and listening practice. This imbalance creates frustration: students may pass N2 yet freeze when asked to introduce themselves casually, write an email, or join in small talk. Solving this requires intentional focus on output. Structured conversation exchanges with native speakers—whether through in-person meetups, online platforms, or tutors—force you to practice producing Japanese under real conditions. Journaling daily, even if short, strengthens writing fluency. Recording yourself speaking about your day helps identify gaps in vocabulary and grammar that passive study cannot reveal. By training both input and output, you ensure that your knowledge is not inert but active, ready to be used spontaneously.

JLPT credentials still carry immense value, but their true power lies in how you leverage them. For university admissions, holding N3 or above signals readiness to handle lectures and coursework. For job applications, N2 often serves as a threshold requirement, while N1 may set you apart in competitive fields. Some companies use JLPT levels to screen applicants, especially for positions that involve translation, customer service, or communication with Japanese clients. Visa applications also benefit: while not always mandatory, JLPT certificates strengthen cases for long-term residency or professional visas by demonstrating tangible integration into Japanese society. The strategic learner understands that the certificate is not just a trophy but a door opener. Presenting it alongside evidence of practical skills—such as writing samples, speaking experience, or relevant work—creates a compelling profile for employers and institutions.

Beyond the external benefits, bridging the JLPT gap transforms your confidence. Passing an exam is satisfying, but speaking to a shop clerk without hesitation, joining a casual chat with colleagues, or understanding a train announcement in real time gives you the sense that Japanese has become part of your life. Certificates measure competence on paper; practical proficiency measures your ability to live the language. The two complement each other, but only together do they create a foundation for true fluency.

## 9.3 Self-Assessment and Progress Tracking

Language learning is often described as a marathon, but unlike a literal race, the path to fluency has no clear finish line visible from the start. The JLPT provides checkpoints, but between those milestones lies long stretches where progress feels invisible. To sustain momentum, learners must develop systems for self-assessment and progress tracking—ways of measuring growth, breaking through plateaus, and celebrating achievements along the way.

One powerful tool is creating a proficiency portfolio. This is more than a notebook of vocabulary lists; it is a living record of your journey. Recording yourself speaking at regular intervals, perhaps once a month, allows you to hear improvements in pronunciation, fluency, and confidence that day-to-day study often obscures. Writing samples, whether diary entries, essays, or mock business emails, reveal how your grammar and vocabulary expand over time. Comprehension logs, where you note what you understood from podcasts, movies, or articles, show incremental gains in listening and reading. Together, these elements provide a multi-dimensional picture of progress, far richer than test scores alone. They also serve as motivation: looking back six months and realizing you can now read a text that once baffled you proves that effort is bearing fruit.

Yet even with careful tracking, many learners hit the dreaded intermediate plateau. After the initial rush of progress, where each week brings visible breakthroughs, growth begins to feel slower. At this stage, learners know enough to function but not enough to feel mastery. Motivation wanes, and some stagnate for years at this level. Overcoming the plateau requires deliberate strategies. One approach is targeted intensive practice periods, where you focus on a specific weakness for a set time. For instance, dedicating a month solely to listening immersion—watching dramas daily, shadowing audio, repeating dialogues—can produce dramatic gains in an area that has stalled. Alternating focus areas keeps learning dynamic, pushing you past stagnation into renewed progress.

Self-awareness plays a critical role here. Plateaus are not signs of failure but signals that your study habits need recalibration. If you have been relying on passive input, shift to active output. If you have been studying alone, join a group or class. If you have been focusing on JLPT drills, dive into novels or podcasts. Each adjustment shakes your brain out of autopilot, forcing it to adapt again. Progress at this stage may not be as dramatic as the beginner's leap, but it is steady and profound, laying the groundwork for advanced fluency.

Celebrating milestones along the way is equally important. Waiting until you achieve N1 or complete a degree program risks discouragement, because those goals may be years away. Instead, create a framework of mini-goals that honor smaller victories. Understanding your first Japanese newspaper article, holding a five-minute conversation without switching to English, writing your first essay entirely in Japanese—each deserves recognition. Celebrations need not be elaborate; treating yourself to a Japanese meal, buying a new book, or simply marking the achievement in your portfolio reinforces motivation. These small rituals remind you that progress is not abstract but tangible, worth acknowledging.

In the long journey to fluency, self-assessment and celebration form the twin supports that keep you moving. The portfolio documents your growth, the plateau strategies push you forward, and the mini-goals sustain your spirit. Combined with external validation from exams like the JLPT, they ensure that your learning is not only measurable but meaningful. Language mastery is never a single moment of arrival; it is a series of steps, tracked, adjusted, and celebrated. By taking ownership of that process, you turn Japanese learning from a vague aspiration into a structured, rewarding journey.

# Chapter 10: Immersion Without Borders – Creating Your Japanese Bubble

*"Students who create 3+ hours of daily Japanese immersion at home achieve conversational fluency 2x faster than those relying solely on formal study."*

## 10.1 Environmental Japanese Saturation

For generations, immersion was considered the privilege of those who could travel or live abroad. Learners believed that only by relocating to Tokyo, Osaka, or Kyoto could they hope to surround themselves with Japanese to the degree necessary for fluency. Today, however, the boundary between home and abroad has thinned. With technology, creativity, and discipline, it is possible to create an immersive environment almost anywhere in the world. Building your own Japanese bubble is not about replicating Japan perfectly but about saturating your daily life with the language until it becomes unavoidable, until your mind begins to process Japanese not as an academic subject but as the background rhythm of existence.

One of the simplest yet most effective techniques is transforming your living space into a language-rich environment. Begin with the objects around you. Label household items with their Japanese names—冷蔵庫 on the refrigerator, 窓 on the window, 机 on the desk. Each glance becomes a flashcard, reinforcing vocabulary without conscious effort. Soon, you no longer think of "refrigerator" but of *reizōko*, not "window" but *mado*. Over time, this subtle shift rewires your brain to associate objects directly with Japanese terms, bypassing translation. This labeling can expand into routines: saying ただいま when you return home, おやすみなさい before bed, until even your private life hums with Japanese rhythm.

Digital devices offer another frontier for immersion. Changing the language settings on your phone, computer, or social media accounts transforms every interaction into practice. Instead of "Settings," you see 設定; instead of "Battery," you see バッテリー. The adjustment may cause frustration at first, but that friction is productive—it forces you to engage actively with Japanese every time you unlock your phone or send a message. Streaming services, online shopping platforms, even video game menus become practice zones. By making Japanese the default language of your digital world, you eliminate the need to carve out separate study time. Your environment itself becomes your teacher.

Creating Japanese-only zones within your living space enhances this effect. Designate areas where only Japanese is allowed your study corner, for instance, or even the kitchen. In these zones, speak to yourself in Japanese, play Japanese media, or write notes exclusively in kana and kanji. The boundary may be artificial, but it creates psychological separation, training your mind to switch into "Japanese mode" on entering. This mental conditioning mirrors the way bilinguals shift between languages depending on environment, eventually making the transition seamless.

Media immersion is the next layer of saturation. Many learners begin with anime, which provides motivation and exposure to natural speech. While valuable, anime alone is insufficient because it often exaggerates speech patterns and leans on stylized vocabulary. A sustainable progression involves moving step by step into more varied content. Japanese variety shows, with their blend of interviews, games, and spontaneous conversations, expose you to colloquial expressions, regional accents, and humor. News programs introduce formal registers, specialized vocabulary, and a steady rhythm of enunciation. Podcasts and audiobooks push comprehension further, requiring you to follow extended discussions without visual cues. Each medium builds on the last, expanding both your ear and your vocabulary while preparing you for the diversity of Japanese as it exists across contexts.

What makes media immersion powerful is not passive consumption but intentional practice. Watching with subtitles at first can support comprehension, but gradually reducing reliance on them forces your brain to listen directly. Rewatching the same content without subtitles deepens recognition, as familiar phrases emerge more clearly. Listening to podcasts during commutes or chores turns idle time into training sessions. Bit by bit, your brain shifts from seeing Japanese as noise to perceiving it as meaning. This transformation cannot be rushed, but it can be nurtured by consistency and progression.

One of the most effective methods for transforming input into active skill is shadowing. This technique involves listening to native speech and repeating it simultaneously, imitating not only words but rhythm, intonation, and even pauses. At first, shadowing feels nearly impossible—voices move too fast, sentences overlap before you finish repeating. But with practice, your tongue and brain adapt. By dedicating focused time blocks to shadowing, you train your muscles and memory together, bridging the gap between listening comprehension and spoken fluency.

The shadowing marathon takes this method further. Instead of brief exercises, learners set aside extended periods—half an hour, an hour, sometimes more—where the sole task is to mimic native speakers continuously. Audiobooks, dramas, or podcasts serve as material. The goal is not perfect accuracy but synchronization, training your voice to ride the same wave as the speaker. Over time, this practice engrains the melody of Japanese into your speech, eliminating the flatness or hesitation that marks many learners. It is exhausting but transformative, forging connections between ear, tongue, and brain that no textbook drill can replicate.

Immersion, however, is not only about the external environment but about mindset. True saturation happens when Japanese is no longer compartmentalized into "study time" but permeates ordinary life. Think in Japanese when planning your day. Describe your surroundings in Japanese while walking. Count money, read signs, or even narrate your thoughts in Japanese. The key is frequency: the more moments you spend engaging with the language, however briefly, the more it becomes woven into your identity. Research consistently shows that learners who create three or more hours of immersion daily achieve fluency twice as fast as those who rely solely on classroom instruction. This is not because three hours magically unlock the brain, but because constant exposure rewires it, shifting Japanese from foreign code to familiar rhythm.

There will be resistance. At first, immersion feels awkward, exhausting, even lonely. Your brain rebels against the effort, craving the ease of your native language. Devices switched into Japanese may confuse you, media without subtitles may overwhelm you, shadowing may frustrate you. Yet it is precisely this struggle that yields growth. Each moment of discomfort is proof that your brain is stretching, adapting to new patterns. Over time, what once felt like resistance becomes routine, and immersion shifts from discipline to habit.

Creating a Japanese bubble is not about isolating yourself from your native world but about infusing your existing world with Japanese until the boundaries blur. Your home, your phone, your media, your thoughts—all become carriers of the language. In doing so, you recreate the essential condition of living abroad without leaving your room. You no longer need to wait for a trip to Japan to experience immersion; you can live in it daily, wherever you are. And when you finally do step into Japan, you will find that the rhythms, phrases, and intonations that once felt foreign now feel like home.

## 10.2 Virtual Exchange and Online Communities

Immersion no longer depends on physical relocation. The internet has dissolved borders, creating opportunities to interact with native speakers, join communities, and build friendships without leaving your own country. For the Japanese learner, this means that meaningful exchange is available every day, provided you know how to structure it and where to find it. The key is not only participation but purposeful participation: crafting online experiences that replicate the unpredictability, rhythm, and intimacy of life in Japan.

One of the most effective tools is language exchange. The premise is simple: two learners, each fluent in a different language, trade time to practice both. Without structure, however, exchanges can drift, leaving both parties frustrated. The most productive model is the 30-30 method: thirty minutes entirely in English, thirty minutes entirely in Japanese. This symmetry ensures balance and prevents one language from dominating. During your thirty minutes of Japanese, resist the temptation to switch into English for clarification; instead, rely on paraphrasing, gestures, or examples. This mimics real-life situations, where you cannot always fall back on translation. Over time, these sessions evolve into friendships where language practice blends seamlessly with genuine conversation, offering not only vocabulary but cultural insight.

Beyond one-on-one exchanges lies the vast world of online communities. Discord servers, Reddit threads, and niche forums offer spaces where Japanese is not a study subject but the medium of discussion. Joining a Japanese Discord dedicated to gaming, for instance, immerses you in slang, teamwork coordination, and real-time banter. Participating in a Reddit community for Japanese literature introduces you to reviews, commentary, and debates conducted entirely in Japanese.

Special interest forums—from anime and manga to cooking, photography, or technology—provide endless opportunities to use the language for real purposes. The benefit is authenticity: you are not practicing contrived dialogues but engaging with Japanese in its natural habitat, shaped by the passions and interests of real speakers.

For those seeking deeper connection, virtual homestay experiences have emerged as a powerful alternative to physical immersion. Platforms like Homestay.com and cultural exchange programs link learners with Japanese families, allowing video calls, cultural lessons, and shared activities that mirror the intimacy of living under the same roof. You might join a family for a virtual dinner, following their conversation as they describe the dishes. You might participate in seasonal traditions—watching a New Year's shrine visit or a summer festival livestreamed from their neighborhood. These interactions go beyond vocabulary; they reveal gestures, habits, and rhythms that cannot be captured in textbooks. For many learners, the bonds formed through these exchanges become as memorable as any trip abroad.

The power of virtual communities lies in continuity. Unlike a two-week vacation, they offer immersion year-round. By logging into a Discord server daily, by checking Japanese Twitter feeds, by chatting weekly with a homestay family, you sustain constant contact with the language. This regularity builds not only fluency but resilience. You learn to handle slang, jokes, and unstructured dialogue. You adapt to different communication styles: the formal politeness of strangers, the casual teasing of friends, the rapid pace of group chats. In doing so, you create an immersion bubble that stretches across time zones, bringing Japan into your daily life.

## 10.3 Maintenance and Lifelong Learning

Fluency, once achieved, is not permanent. Like muscles, language skills atrophy without use. Many learners who once passed N2 or N1 discover, after years without practice, that their comprehension has dulled, their vocabulary shrunk, their confidence vanished. The question then becomes not only how to reach fluency but how to maintain it across a lifetime. The answer lies in recognizing the minimum effective dose, rotating skills deliberately, and engaging in the teaching-learning cycle that cements knowledge through sharing.

The minimum effective dose refers to the smallest daily practice that keeps your Japanese alive. Research and experience suggest that around thirty minutes of focused engagement per day is sufficient to maintain proficiency. This might be a podcast during your commute, a journal entry before bed, or a chat with a friend online. Thirty minutes ensures that Japanese remains active in your mental circuits, preventing decay. Anything beyond that accelerates improvement, but consistency matters more than volume. Sporadic bursts of five hours cannot replace the steady habit of half an hour daily. In this way, maintenance becomes sustainable, woven into routine rather than requiring heroic effort.

Even with regular practice, skills risk becoming unbalanced. A learner who reads novels daily but never speaks may maintain literacy while losing oral fluency. Someone who practices conversation often but neglects writing may falter when asked to compose emails or reports. Preventing such atrophy requires a rotation schedule. By alternating focus between reading, writing, listening, and speaking, you keep each domain alive. One week might emphasize listening—immersing in dramas, news, or podcasts. Another might focus on writing—composing essays, emails, or even social media posts in Japanese. Rotating skills not only preserves balance but also prevents boredom, keeping learning fresh through variety.

Perhaps the most powerful strategy for lifelong learning is entering the teaching-learning cycle. Explaining Japanese concepts to beginners, whether through tutoring, blogs, or casual advice, forces you to clarify your own understanding. When you explain why に and で differ, or how humble verbs function, you confront gaps you may not have noticed. Teaching requires precision, and in preparing explanations, you deepen your mastery. Moreover, the act of guiding others creates community, reinforcing motivation. You are no longer only a learner but a contributor, part of the chain that passes knowledge forward.

This cycle of teaching also transforms perspective. Beginners often ask questions that reveal subtleties advanced learners overlook. For example, a novice might ask why 日本に行く means "go to Japan" but 日本で行く shifts the nuance entirely. Answering this requires more than rote memory—it requires internalized understanding. In articulating such distinctions, you solidify your grasp and ensure it will not fade. Over time, teaching becomes less about repeating rules and more about sharing insights, enriching both teacher and student.

Lifelong learning also means embracing change. Language evolves, and Japanese is no exception. New slang, abbreviations, and cultural references emerge constantly, especially in online spaces. Staying fluent requires remaining curious, engaging with current media, and accepting that mastery is never complete. Reading contemporary novels, following Japanese YouTubers, or engaging with online forums keeps you connected to the living language rather than a static version frozen in textbooks.

Maintenance, then, is not a burden but a practice of integration. By setting a minimum daily dose, rotating skills, and embracing the teaching-learning cycle, you ensure that Japanese remains a living part of your identity. Instead of fearing loss, you cultivate growth that adapts with you across the years. Fluency becomes less a destination and more a companion, a language that walks beside you through shifting contexts, ready whenever you need it.

# Conclusion: Living the Language, Becoming the Speaker

Every journey has an end point, but language learning resists such neat closure. Japanese is not a mountain you climb once, plant your flag on, and then descend victorious. It is more like a landscape you come to inhabit—a terrain that shifts with the seasons, opens new paths as you explore, and deepens in meaning the longer you stay. To conclude a book on Japanese mastery is not to say, "Now you are finished," but to remind you that mastery is a process, one that continues long after exams are passed, conversations flow, and novels can be read without translation.

The path you have traveled through these chapters has offered you structure, milestones, and techniques. From learning the mechanics of hiragana and katakana to building complex sentences with particles and verb conjugations, you have seen how Japanese can be understood piece by piece. You have also glimpsed how culture, context, and subtlety permeate every utterance, teaching you that language is never divorced from the people who use it. Along the way, you've encountered the JLPT roadmap, digital tools, immersion methods, and cultural codes that reveal how Japanese is lived both on the street and online. Each element has been another tool placed in your hands, another perspective to help you move forward with confidence.

Yet the real conclusion is this: you cannot learn Japanese passively. Mastery emerges not from reading about techniques but from applying them relentlessly in your own life. This means choosing to speak even when you stumble, to listen even when you understand only fragments, to write even when your sentences feel clumsy. It means accepting mistakes as proof that you are using the language rather than just studying it. Every time you engage actively, you push Japanese out of the realm of theory and into the realm of lived experience.

One of the most liberating truths about Japanese is that you never have to wait until you are "ready." You are ready now, even if your vocabulary is small and your grammar fragile. You can greet someone, order food, send a message, or comment on a video today. Fluency does not arrive suddenly, as if a switch flips; it grows imperceptibly from thousands of such small moments. The conversations you attempt now, however imperfect, lay the groundwork for the effortless fluency you will one day enjoy. To postpone speaking until you feel prepared is to delay the very practice that makes you prepared.

At the same time, patience is essential. Japanese is a long game. The scripts demand discipline, the grammar demands adjustment, the cultural codes demand sensitivity. There will be weeks when you feel progress racing ahead, and months when it seems to stall. This rhythm is natural. Plateaus are not signs of failure but of consolidation, moments when your brain integrates what it has absorbed before it leaps forward again. Trust this process. Consistency, not speed, is what brings results. Ten minutes of practice daily over years will transform you more than sporadic bursts of effort.

Immersion remains the most powerful accelerator. Whether through labeling your home, saturating your devices with Japanese, or joining online communities, the more you surround yourself with the language, the faster it becomes second nature. Immersion teaches you not only words and grammar but rhythm, intonation, humor, and etiquette. It exposes you to the living language in all its messiness—unfinished sentences, slang, dialects, and expressions that never appear in textbooks. In that messiness lies fluency. To master Japanese is to learn how to live inside its unpredictability and to thrive there.

But do not confuse mastery with perfection. Even native speakers make mistakes, forget kanji, or stumble over formal expressions. The goal is not flawlessness but confidence: the ability to communicate, to connect, to continue speaking even when your words are not perfect. Confidence grows not from avoiding mistakes but from surviving them, from discovering that communication continues even when grammar falters. You will be surprised how far goodwill, effort, and humility carry you in Japanese interactions.

Another essential lesson is that language is inseparable from people. Japanese is not just a system of sounds and symbols—it is a living thread that binds communities. To study it in isolation is to miss its essence. Seek out conversation partners, friends, mentors, and communities. Each exchange will teach you something that no textbook can. Through people you learn the *honne* and *tatemae*, the play of particles in casual chat, the emotional shading of sentence-ending particles like ね or よ. Through people you discover that Japanese is not just spoken— it is laughed, whispered, sung, and written in ways that reflect the infinite variety of human expression.

If you ever feel discouraged, return to your reasons for beginning. Perhaps you dreamed of reading manga in the original, of traveling in Japan without relying on English, of working in a Japanese company, or of connecting with a friend or loved one. Whatever your spark was, keep it alive. Revisit it when kanji overwhelm you, when listening feels impossible, when motivation falters. That spark will remind you that Japanese is not an abstract task but a deeply personal pursuit.

This journey is also about identity. As you grow in Japanese, you will discover not only new words but new ways of being. You may find parts of yourself that express differently in Japanese than in your native language. You may discover patience in waiting for the right particle, attentiveness in noticing pauses, humility in apologizing with the proper form. Japanese does not just add to your skillset; it shapes your worldview. It teaches that silence can be communication, that respect can be encoded in grammar, that relationships matter as much as facts. In learning Japanese, you do not simply add another tongue—you expand your humanity.

So where do you go from here? The answer is simple: forward. Set your next milestone, whether it is mastering N4, joining a Japanese Discord server, finishing your first novel, or making a phone call in Japanese. Track your progress, celebrate small victories, and adjust your methods as needed. Do not be afraid to make the language part of your daily identity, whether through journaling, shadowing, or chatting online. Let Japanese flow into your routines until it feels less like a study subject and more like a natural part of your life.

Remember too that mastery has no finish line. Even if you achieve N1, even if you live in Japan for years, you will continue to learn. New slang emerges, cultural contexts shift, and your own goals evolve. Fluency is not a static state but a lifelong relationship with the language. The beauty of Japanese is that it always has more to offer: deeper literature, richer conversation, subtler cultural insight. Your task is not to conquer it once and for all but to keep walking, to remain a learner even as you become fluent.

As you close this book, know that your journey has only begun. You carry with you the strategies, insights, and structures to move forward with confidence. But the real work happens outside these pages—in the words you speak today, the sentences you write tomorrow, the conversations you stumble through and the ones you triumph in. Each of those moments is a brick in the foundation of your mastery.

Japanese is waiting for you—not as a test to pass, but as a companion to live with. Every word you learn is another step across the bridge that connects you to new people, new ideas, and new parts of yourself. Walk it steadily. Walk it bravely. And one day, without realizing it, you will look back and see how far you have come, how the foreign has become familiar, and how the language you once studied has become the language you live.

www.ingramcontent.com/pod-product-compliance
Lightning Source LLC
Chambersburg PA
CBHW061959220426
43662CB00011B/1744